HELP!

I've Turned Into My Mother

HELP!

I've Turned Into My Mother

ReShonda Tate Billingsley

SBI

STREBOR BOOKS

NEW YORK   LONDON   TORONTO   SYDNEY

Strebor Books
P.O. Box 6505
Largo, MD 20792
http://www.streborbooks.com

Cover design: www.mariondesigns.com

ISBN-13 978-1-59309-050-0
ISBN-10   1-59309-050-1
LCCN 2005920190

First Strebor Books trade paperback edition November 2005

10   9   8   7   6   5   4   3   2   1

Manufactured in the United States of America

For information regarding special discounts for bulk purchases, please contact Simon & Schuster Special Sales at 1-800-456-6798 or business@simonandschuster.com

For the mothers of the world, especially mine, Nancy B.

*"For I am my mother's daughter,
and the drums of Africa still beat in my heart."*
—MARY McLEOD BETHUNE, educator and activist

ACKNOWLEDGMENTS

I must first and foremost thank my own mother who molded and shaped me into the woman I am today; who I know will be understanding about me "telling the whole world our business"; and who I know loves me unconditionally. I'm honored to say I'm just like you.

To my husband, Miron, who as usual supported my dreams and pushed me to write, even when I didn't feel like writing.

To my sister, Tanisha, who helped me recall all those wonderful stories about us growing up and who is turning into our mother, too (although she'll never admit it).

To the absolute best publicist in the nation, Angie Pickett Henderson of Adeeva Publicity. Thank you for working tirelessly on my behalf. When you blow up, remember I knew you when.

To my wonderful agent, Sara Camilli, who continues to believe and support my work.

To the woman who truly has it goin' on, the unstoppable Zane. Thank you for not only allowing me to share my work with the world, but for supporting me when I was just starting out. Much thanks also to Charmaine and the whole Strebor staff.

Thank you to all the wonderful people at Simon & Schuster, including two of the best editors in the business, Selena James and Brigitte Smith.

Of course, a huge, huge thank you to all the wonderful women who shared their stories—the mothers and the daughters. Much love to the men who weren't afraid to share their stories as well. Thank you all for opening your hearts and souls. You'll never know all the lives you touch.

Thank you to all my sorors, friends, relatives, colleagues, bookclubs, bookstores and literary buddies. You all have helped me achieve my dreams.

TABLE OF CONTENTS

TOP 5 WAYS YOU KNOW
YOU'VE TURNED INTO YOUR MOTHER

5. You call your child from the other room to change the channel on the TV that's sitting two feet in front of you.

4. You tell your child, "Shut up, before I give you something to cry about!"

3. You yell for your children to close the doors because they're "letting all the air out."

2. You can't go to sleep until you know your child is tucked safely in bed.

1. You spit on your thumb, then wipe something off your child's face.

MOTHER WIT

Chances are your mother said it. Or her mother said it. Or you know someone who has a mother who said it—those crazy quotes you could say in unison. In surveying more than five-hundred women for this book, the following sayings kept popping up. Is something your mother said here? Or here's the real question: do you now spew your own mother wit?

"Gimmie got his neck broke messing with his kinfolk."

"I'm going to see a man about a dog."

"If all your friends jump off a building, will you?"

"I ain't your friend. I'm your mama."

"Make sure you have clean underwear on, in case you get into an accident."

"Why would he buy the cow, if he is getting the milk for free?"

"You don't have a pot to piss in or a window to throw it out of."

"You better eat everything on your plate; there are people starving in Africa."

INTRODUCTION

You may be a grown-up woman—married, single, satisfied with who you are or still trying to find yourself—but you are still your mother's daughter. Deny it. You can try. Defy it. You can try that, too. At some point, though, you will acknowledge that your mother has had, and still has, a big influence on you.

Growing up, my mother got on my last nerve. I'm not ashamed to admit it. I loved her, but she drove me crazy. To me, she was the meanest mother in the world. She made me come in the house when the street lights came on (while all my friends were still hanging outside); she made me come home from dates by ten p.m. (when everybody else could stay out until midnight and one a.m.). To this day I still have nightmares about the time my mother showed up at a teen club (in her pink hair rollers) and had the deejay announce for me to "bring my behind on." Back then, if you were to ask me how I was mothered, I'd tell you "badly."

I'm not ashamed to admit how I felt about my mother then...because I have such appreciation and respect for her now. I can't tell you how many times I heard, "You'll thank me for this one day." I do.

Many mother/daughter books on the market today will give a textbook examination of our relationships with our mothers. They'll look at our lives as toddlers—exploring how we threw temper tantrums because Mommy wouldn't buy us some candy. They'll dissect our teen years—when we screamed things like "I hate you!" to our mothers and ordered them to "respect our privacy." Well, I don't know about you, but I definitely *can't* relate.

When my mother said no, she meant no. A temper tantrum only meant you would get your butt beat—right there in the candy aisle. And I shudder just thinking about what my mom would do if I ever screamed, "I hate you!" (She'd probably do ten to twenty in a maximum-security facility for attempted murder.) No, for me, and most of the girlfriends I talked to for this book, things just didn't work like that.

See, our mothers are unique. A loving-nurturing-but-still-don't-play type of uniqueness. That's why I decided to write this book. To explore the complexities—the good, the bad, and the ugly—of our relationships with our mothers. And to find a way to improve those relationships, even those that we believe may need no improvement.

It is my hope that the book will prove beneficial to mothers and daughters from all walks of life. Because regardless of race, chances are you'll see yourself, or your mother, somewhere in these pages.

At some time or another, almost all of us see our mothers in ourselves and cringe. If you would've told me I had turned into my mother ten years ago, I probably would've tried to cut you. Call it maturity or whatever, but today I would take that as the sincerest form of flattery. Don't get me wrong. My mother has some issues. She'll probably curse me out just for writing this, complaining that I'm "telling the whole world her business." But that's just one of the things I learned to appreciate about her. That's what I hope you walk away with. The ability to appreciate and grow from the good *and* the bad of your own relationship with your mother or daughter.

By no means is this book designed to give you a clinical or psychological analysis of your relationship with your mother. It's simply an avenue of discussion among girlfriends. Hopefully, some of the stories the women here so graciously share will help you build a stronger foundation so that when someone tells you that you've turned into your mother, your reply will simply be, "Why, thank you."

PART I

Oh my God,
I'm just like Mama!

Chapter One *Because I said so!*

"I grew up in a predominantly middle-class suburban neighborhood and I would watch as all my suburban girlfriends inquisitively asked their mothers question after question. They got patient, loving responses. My mom's response every time I'd ask her 'why'–'Because I said so!'"

— CARLA, *twenty-seven*

Like Carla, "Because I said so" was a staple in my mother's conversations. It was the answer to every question from "Why is the sky blue?" to "Why can't I go outside?" Every now and then, my mother would feel a little patient and I'd get some actual answers. But generally, I had a three-question limit before she reverted to her standard response of "Because I said so!"

I hated those four little words and vowed that if I ever had children, I would be loving and patient. I would understand my child's inquisitive nature. I would answer my child's endless questions no matter what.

Yeah, right.

That lasted until my first daughter could fully form sentences. Don't get me wrong. I tried. I really did. But one day, after trying five times to calmly explain to my two-year-old that a chocolate chip cookie would ruin her dinner, that childhood promise went out the window. It was the last time that did it. Her repeated question was like the small spark that sets off the fireworks on the Fourth of July. Her tiny, whining voice, drawing the question out, "Buuuttt mommmyeeee, why can't I have the cookie?"

I lost it and simply yelled, "Because I said so!"

And you know what? It worked. She shrugged, stuck her bottom lip out, then quietly went back to watching *Rugrats*.

I was standing in front of the mirror at the time. When I looked up, I saw my mother and gasped. The reflection in the mirror smiled. A cunning, I-told-you-so smile. It was eerie. But it would be one of many times my mother would creep into my psyche.

My girlfriend, twenty-seven-year-old Carla, remembers similar experiences.

"My mother was the queen of 'because-I-said-so's.' I used to think she was like a god or something since the snow was white because she said so. Night turned to day because she said so. Rain made you wet because she said so. At first I was in awe, then as I got older, that started to drive me crazy. I felt like my mother just didn't want to be bothered with my questions," Carla says.

But Carla says with adulthood has come clarity.

"In my suburban neighborhood, I would watch my friends' relationships with their mothers and wonder why my mother couldn't be as patient in responding to my questions. What I didn't understand then, that I do now, is my mother was a single, working mom. She would work nine-hour days, then come home to care for me and my siblings. So I guess the last thing she felt like doing was answering a hundred meaningless questions from her three children. Many of my friends' mothers didn't work, and if they did it wasn't a matter of die-hard necessity like it was for my family. So they were a lot more tolerant of their children. I'm not saying that makes it right, but I definitely understand," Carla says.

For thirty-two-year-old Tammy, "because I said so" has become a staple in her vocabulary simply because her four-year-old daughter challenges everything she says. Just like Tammy says she did her mother.

"I've turned into my mother and my daughter has turned into me." Tammy laughed. "I used to do the exact same thing to my mother. If she said two plus two was four, I would ask why. My mother would try to explain that that was just the way math worked. I'd keep asking why and she'd finally snap, 'Because I said so!' My daughter now does that to me. And I respond just like my mother, by saying 'Because I said so!'"

DO AS I SAY, NOT AS I DO

My parents divorced when I was ten years old and I would've bet my Wonder Woman Underoos that my mother lived a celibate life. My sister and I never saw any men traipsing in and out of our home. The only man we ever saw my mother with would later become our stepfather. So imagine my surprise when, as an adult, my mother shared how she was "getting her groove on" back then. After getting over the initial shock that my mother actually had sex with someone other than my father (and that was only tolerable because they needed to create me), it brought a new level of respect for me. My mother respected her position and chose to exhibit standards by which she wanted us to live. Too often in child-rearing, mothers tell their daughters, "Do as I say, not as I do."

"It sends conflicting messages," says thirty-nine-year-old Jacqueline. "My mom would tell me how I needed to stay away from drugs...all the while she's shooting up. She'd give me this spiel about wanting better for me and I'm looking at her high ass like, you've got to be kidding me. I got hooked on drugs myself. And I think—no, I know—it started from me sneaking some of my mother's weed when I was only thirteen years old. While I know my drug problems are my responsibility, I blamed her for my drug addiction because she wasn't setting any kind of example, and it totally destroyed our relationship."

Even though most children raised in traditional homes are taught the importance of honesty, the lesson is undermined when parents are not honest. Growing up, many of us saw that grown folks didn't always practice what they preached. Many didn't exhibit the same honesty they told us was so important. Or, many times, we would tell the "truth" only to be punished for such talk.

"I remember I got my behind tore up," says twenty-seven-year-old Veronica. "I told our next-door neighbor that the casserole she had given us tasted horrible. My mother slapped the taste out of my mouth, then beat my behind. I couldn't understand it because she was the one who had talked about how nasty it was. I was just being truthful because it was God-awful. But after that, and to this day, I just keep my mouth shut and don't say anything in situations like that."

Of the more than five-hundred women surveyed for this book, seventy-six percent say they were pleased with the way they were raised. At the time though, most say they didn't understand/appreciate/respect the way they were mothered. It took becoming adults, even mothers themselves, for that transformation to take effect.

There were some women who endured physical, mental and emotional abuse...they had different perspectives on the way they were mothered. Many said their current relationships were strained by their mother's failure to protect them as a child. But overall, most agreed that their mothers are by nature strong and loving; they simply have different ways of showing it.

One of the main ways some mothers say they show their love is by providing. Patricia Hill Collins, noted women's studies lecturer, writes that one of the central concepts of motherhood is being a provider. She writes: "Mothers experience the dual goals of needing to help their daughters survive physically, yet wanting to encourage them to transcend the boundaries with which they are confronted. Mothers, who are often described as 'strong disciplinarians and overly protective parents,' succeed in raising self-reliant and assertive daughters."

But for some women, that providing comes at a price.

"My mother and I don't have an extremely close relationship. Growing up she was never there. She was always at work," thirty-three-year-old Sonya says. "I resented her for it. Now I see myself doing the exact same thing with my three kids. But I have to work two jobs just to support us because their father isn't around. I guess my mom probably said the same thing."

These days, many women, particularly black women, are trained early with the notion that they must work to support themselves and their families. Several researchers who describe the important role mothers play in raising their daughters have found that today's mothers rear their daughters to be economically independent, strong, self-confident and capable of handling family responsibilities. They tend to place less emphasis on cultivating stereotypical qualities of femininity and more emphasis on encouraging a combination of self-sufficiency and the traditional roles of childcare.

"I went to a predominantly white university and I was absolutely amazed at the number of women who were there simply to find a good husband. That never crossed my mind," says twenty-nine-year-old Tammy.

The vast majority of minority women in the United States know in girlhood that they will be workers. In *Hard Times Cotton Mill Girls,* author Katie Geneva Cannon remembers: "It was always assumed that we would work. Work was a given in life, almost like breathing and sleeping. I'm always surprised when I hear people talking about somebody taking care of them, because we always knew that we were going to work."

Like older generations of women who struggled, we were taught not only that we would be workers, but there was to be no "shame" in our game. We did whatever it took to make ends meet.

Those women who are major providers in their households, both in those where men are present and where they are not, often feel it is up to them to keep it all together. The women work, then return home to what sociologist Arlie Hochschild calls, "the second shift," that is housework and childcare, often without the help of male partners.

"I think that's where I got my work ethic," says thirty-five-year-old Kia. "My mother has always done whatever it took to put food on the table. No job was beneath her. I feel the same way. I'm an accountant by trade, but if I need to go work at McDonald's to feed my son, I'll do it without hesitation."

For women in general, it's been about making a better life. But Patricia Hill Collins says for black women in particular, it's about a better life *and* surviving.

"The black woman has had to implement survival skills since her days on the plantation," Hill Collins says. "So mothers, by nature, pass those survival skills on to their daughters."

The mothers I interviewed, black, white and brown, say they have supported their daughters, pushed them to succeed, and have set high expectations for them, in part because high levels of achievement are more possible than ever before. In *Overcoming the Odds,* Marcia Gamble writes, "Each generation sets higher expectations than the preceding one. Many of these mothers were themselves expected to attend college, even though their mothers did not. These mothers expected their daughters to go to graduate school."

"My mom cleaned houses," says forty-four-year-old Ida. "She was determined that I would not follow in her footsteps. She swore if anything, someone would be cleaning my house. She wanted me to have a better life. She was strict, so much so, that growing up, I hated her. But I see now what she was trying to do."

Jada, who is now an ob/gyn, plans to push her daughter the way her mother pushed her, even though she knows that may be an exceptionally high standard.

"I want my six-year-old daughter to have an even better life than me," she says.

But it's important to find a balance, Hill Collins says. Many mothers were never afforded the opportunity to pursue prominent careers and by the time those doors began opening up, they were not equipped with the skills nor the time or money to go back to school and acquire those skills. So instead, many focused their energies on making sure their children could go through doors they couldn't. But mothers today—the doctors, lawyers, etc.—pushing their child to even higher standards may find their plans backfiring.

"Every generation of mothers has wanted their children to live better than they did," adds sixty-three-year-old Ruby Hicks. "My grandmother simply wanted my mother to have babies and be a good wife and mother. Education was never an option. Then my mother just wanted me to learn a trade, be a secretary or a nurse. And I wanted my daughter to shoot for the stars. I pushed her to pursue an advanced degree, which she has. Something like that was unheard of for my mother."

Even those women who don't yet have children say the way they were mothered plays a critical role in all aspects of their lives.

"I was raised in the church. I'm talking *in* the church," says Shannon Adams. "We were there for Monday night business meeting; Tuesday night choir rehearsal; Wednesday night Bible study; Thursday night youth choir rehearsal; Friday women's ministry meeting; and Saturday, choir rehearsal again. And Sunday, from sun-up to sundown. My mother shoved religion down my throat. Now as an adult, while I believe in God, I just can't stand going to church."

For some women, it's the things they *didn't* get that strained their childhoods.

"My mother never showed us any affection. Her mother didn't show her any. I know without a doubt, how much my mother loves me—even though

I can't ever recall her telling me. But there's nothing like having your mother actually tell you, or show you in some other way than just bringing home food to put on the table. I know some people—my mother included—who think that that should be enough, but it's not. That's what I grew up with, though. I'm really scared that when I have children I'll continue the cycle," says twenty-four-year-old Tangie.

The first step in making sure that doesn't happen, says Texas therapist Dr. Victoria Sloan, is for Tangie to sit down and talk with her mother about her feelings. "Oftentimes in our community, we brush things under the rug. Certain things just aren't discussed. And hurts our mother caused us is at the top of that list. But just because we don't address it, doesn't mean it goes away. In fact, it most likely will continue to fester—eventually hindering healthy relationships," Dr. Sloan says.

Cali believes that's just what happened to her. "My relationship with my mother is very strained. We hardly talk and I like it that way. She was a very cold, demanding mother; and when I became an adult, I just found it easier to not talk to her than to try and change her."

Therapist Patricia Reid-Merritt finds that the mothers she talks to describe motherhood as their most significant role.

"These mothers view their parenting as being a part of a heritage and serving to link the children to their past, present, and future. This is the tapestry of experiences that these mothers weave when raising their children."

REFLECTIONS

❧ Do you think your mother believes she did a good job raising you? Do you agree?

❧ Are some of your actions as an adult a rebellion from your mother's actions when you were a child?

❧ What emotion is most prevalent when you think of your childhood with your mother?

Chapter Two *The face in the mirror*

"My mother had this yellow-flowered muumuu housedress that she used to wear. I couldn't for the life of me understand how anyone of sane mind would wear a contraption like that. That was twenty-five years ago. I now have one in purple. It's the most comfortable thing I've ever worn."

—Shelly, *thirty-six*

I don't know about you, but I'm guilty of it. Scores of my girlfriends are guilty of it. It's not something we're proud of, but with maturity, we're willing to admit it. We've metamorphosed into our mothers in more ways than one.

For Shelly, it's with the clothes.

"In addition to the muumuu housedress, Mama used to wear nothing but cotton underclothes. Her bra and panties never matched. In fact, her panties looked like big sheets. I wondered how Daddy could even still find her attractive and vowed that when I grew up, I would never dress like that. After about five years of marriage, I realized cotton really is comfortable," Shelly says.

Shelly says she does still, from time to time, try to look sexy for her husband, but "between working all the time, keeping the house, and raising the kids, matching underwear just dropped to the bottom of my list."

Growing up, Melanie watched her mother "nag" everyone in sight.

"It was nerve-wrecking. 'Do this, do that, pick up this, pick up that. Where are you going? Why are you going?' Not just me, but everyone. It drove my father crazy," she says.

But guess who's doing the nagging now?

"I think the first time I realized I was turning in to my mother was in college, when I found myself constantly nagging my boyfriend. One day, he just got so frustrated and snapped, 'You're acting like somebody's mother!' I was stunned because I *was* acting like someone's mother—mine."

Melanie says she now makes a conscious effort to keep the nagging at a minimum.

"My mother is really a sweet person. I just hate that I picked up the most negative trait she possesses. I have to really work on that," Melanie says.

For me, T-day (Transformation Day) became noticeable through something as simple as picking up my mother's quirky sayings.

I remember one Saturday when I was about eleven years old. My family had piled into our old 1973 station wagon. I excitedly asked, "Hey, Ma, where are we going?"

"To see a man about a dog," she replied.

Thirty minutes later, we ended up at the mall. I thought, "Oh wow, we're headed to the pet store." We went to Dillard's department store, Palais Royal and a host of other stores, but never the pet store.

The next weekend it was the same thing.

"Mama, where are we going?"

"To see a man about a dog," she casually said as we got into the car.

I smiled, thinking, "Okay, finally, we're going to get our dog."

We never did get that dog. Eventually, my mother explained to me that that was just a saying; we were never *literally* going to get a dog. At the time I thought that was the dumbest thing I had ever heard. Why would you say you're going to see a man about a dog if you weren't really going to see a man about a dog?

That wasn't the only quirky saying my mother loved spouting. There was "If I do, then Popeye's a punk" (don't even ask); "You 'bout ate up with the dumb ass" (can't explain that one either, but I think that meant I was doing something stupid); and "While you saying, 'scat, scat,' someone is around the corner saying, 'Here kitty, kitty'" (that one meant that you have to take care of your man at home.)

After hearing all of those sayings I thought, no doubt about it, my mother is really crazy. So imagine my surprise when I was driving with a group of friends one day and one of them started backseat driving.

"Turn here! Watch that car! You're going too fast!" a friend bellowed.

I calmly turned to her and said, "Look, I'm screwing this cat. If I have any luck, I'll give you some kittens."

Every eye in the car was on me, looking on in disbelief.

"What the hell did you just say?" my girlfriend Raqqi asked.

I repeated it without hesitation. "I said, 'I'm screwing this cat. If I have any luck, I'll give you some kittens.'"

"What in the world does that mean?" my friend Clemelia asked.

"It means I'm driving and if I need your help, I'll let you know," I replied.

"So why didn't you just say that?" Raqqi said as she shook her head.

I just kind of laughed, until Raqqi, who knows my mother well, said, "That sounds just like something your mother would say."

I almost ran off the road when she said that. She was right. In fact, that was one of my mother's favorite sayings. How had what I once called a "cocka-mamie phrase" dare pass through my lips? I drove in stunned silence as realization crept over me.

I think that day was the beginning of my transformation. There would be many more days when I'd spew some oddball saying that oftentimes took some explaining before anyone got its meaning. For me, that was a true sign that I'd turned into my mother.

My thirty-one-year-old girlfriend Lynn says she's picked up her mother's early morning habits—something she never thought she'd do.

"My mother used to wake up at the crack of dawn every day, like four forty-five every morning. I used to think the lady was nuts! She didn't have to report to work until seven-thirty. She would wake us up to make sure we had breakfast and to see what we had on to go to school. Then she'd leave for work. The bus wouldn't pick us up for another two hours! During the summertime, kids dreamed of sleeping in. Not my mama's kids. She would come in at nine a.m. and open the blinds right in your face and say, 'Wake up! You are not gonna sleep all day!' (I thought this had to have been a mild form of child abuse because ALL of my friends were allowed to sleep until like eleven or twelve.) She told us that sleeping late would make us lazy. Oh my, how I thought she was nuts," Lynn says. "Now, as I call my friends early in the morning (six a.m.) and sense attitude in their voice, I wonder, what is wrong with my friends? Doesn't everyone get up at 6 a.m. like I do? ...And then I realize...dammit! I have turned into my mother."

Carolyn's realization that she was turning into her mother came like a thief in the night, she says. Quickly and without warning.

"I woke up one day and my mother's cellulite had found its way onto my thighs," she says. "My mother is short, five-feet-two and about 240 pounds. I'm short, too, but vowed never to be overweight. When I was in college I was obsessive about what I ate for that very reason. But after my first baby, before I knew it, I looked just like her. No matter what I did or didn't eat, no matter how much I exercised, I couldn't get the weight off. Even my doctor told me while I could tone up, for the most part, it was genetic. It was bad enough that I had her personality; now I had her body."

Forty-nine-year-old Lena admits to having her mother's body, but it's one thing you won't find her complaining about.

"Growing up, it used to bug the heck out of me when my male friends would salivate all over my mother, always talking about how fine she was. She dressed all sexy, nothing over the top, but enough that everybody could see how perfectly sculpted her body was. Now that I'm grown and built just like her, I understand. Because, baby, I'm pushing forty and I still got it. And believe me, I want everybody to know it. Hence, the tight Hilfiger jeans," Lena says.

My friend Shannon laughs when she thinks of the little things she's picked up from her mother and thought she'd never do.

"Oh, my God. I am so my mother. She used to go shopping, then hide the bags from my dad in the trunk of the car. I do that now (you don't think my husband will read this, huh?) My mom used to also belt out songs even though she couldn't sing a lick and didn't know the words. I do the exact same thing now," Shannon says.

Forty-seven-year-old Marie says while she recoils in fear at the prospect of becoming her mother, it's something her mother actually relishes.

"My mother told me that I sound just like her on the telephone. She says that like it's a good thing," Marie says. "While I cringe at the thought, she finds it quite funny."

For forty-one-year-old Tangie, T-day came when she gave birth to her first child. And with it, a newfound sense of appreciation.

"My mother was always so strict. I never could understand it and hated it when I was younger. But the day I had my baby, I looked at her and said, I don't care how mad she gets at me, I'm going to do everything I can to keep her safe. And if that means being strict and having her mad at me, so be it. My mother looked at me as I held my child, and although no words were exchanged, her eyes seemed to say, 'Maybe now, you can finally understand.' And I do, believe me I do."

REFLECTIONS

❧ What is the trait you possess that you would say most resembles your mother?

❧ Would you consider turning into your mother a good or bad thing? Why?

❧ What are some things your mother used to do that you swore you would never do? Do you find yourself doing any of those things now?

CHAPTER THREE *Mother knows best?*

"My mother is a she-devil, put on this earth to make my life a living hell. She thinks, no let me correct that, she knows, that she is an expert on every subject. Why I'm not married? She has it all figured out. What's wrong with the world today? She can tell you in sixty seconds. Hell, let her tell it, she even knows where Osama Bin Laden is."

—CASEY, *twenty-six*

Casey readily admits that her relationship with her mother is strained. They simply do not get along.

"She's a know-it-all," Casey says. "She is an evil, evil woman. And our relationship works best when we never talk."

Harsh? Maybe, Casey admits. "But it's the way I feel and I'm not going to sugarcoat it," she says.

Casey says the root of all her problems with her mother stems from the fact that "she thinks she knows everything. Nothing I do is right. She never sees my point about anything and she's always putting me down, trying to tell me how to run my life. It's nerve-wrecking," she says.

Diane admits she and her mother don't get along because they are too much alike.

"We're both stubborn and steadfast. And I was one of those rebellious types. My mother would tell me not to do something, and I would do it just because she told me not to," Diane says.

I know the mothers out there reading this are probably saying we simply don't like to listen. In some cases, they're right. But what our mothers need to understand is that we're coming into our own, and sometimes that means you have to let us do things—even fail—on our own. And it's imperative that you respect our choices.

Take my situation with the birth of my first child for instance. I read every baby book under the sun. I surfed the Internet, joined Yahoo groups, did everything and anything I could to learn how to be a better mom.

So when I saw my mother about to feed my four-month-old some mashed-up collard greens and cornbread, I freaked.

"What are you doing?!" I yelled.

"What does it look like? This baby looks hungry. She needs some meat on her bones," my mother said as she rocked little Mya back and forth. "It's just collards. Good grief!"

"Mother!" I said, snatching the plate of greens from her. "She is not supposed to eat solid foods!"

My mother looked at me like I was crazy. "Says who?"

"All the doctors. Every book I read. They all said you don't give a baby solids this young," I replied.

My mother rolled her eyes and snatched the plate back. "Greens ain't go'n hurt this baby. I gave you collards, mustards, turnips, even put pot liquor in your bottles and you turned out just fine," she snapped as she mashed up more greens, then fed Mya with her fingers.

I sighed in frustration. How I raised my child was a constant battle between me and my mother, who didn't get why I needed to consult a book, or that "stupid computer" to find out how to take care of my kid. She felt she knew best because after all, she had "raised two girls who weren't on drugs, serial killers or hookers."

"That's the same story with my mother," added my girlfriend Tara. "My mother and I had a big blow-up when I caught her letting my one-year-old take a sip of her wine cooler. I almost had a heart attack. She didn't see what the big deal was, saying it wasn't but a drop and it was cute. I swear, I wanted to have my mother arrested that day."

"Tara's daddy used to let her drink some of his beer all the time. These mamas today just make a big deal out of everything. It wasn't nothing but a little wine," Tara's mother, Billie, said. "And guess what, it didn't kill her or turn her into a raving alcoholic."

Maybe not, but Toronto therapist Carole-Anne Vatcher says mothers have to give their daughters breathing room.

"You have to let your daughter make her own life decisions. Even if you disagree with them. Let her make her own mistakes and find her own way through tough situations. Just make sure she knows you're supportive," Vatcher says.

When I announced to my mother that I was taking a fifteen thousand-dollar pay cut, leaving Houston and moving to a small town so I could pursue a career as a television news anchor, she told me I had lost my mind.

"But I'm following my dreams, Mama," I told her.

"Yeah, whatever. Why can't you dream here in Houston?"

"Because in the news business, you have to go work in a small market, then work your way back up to the big city," I replied.

"Who came up with that dumb rule?" my mother responded.

"I don't know. I don't make the rules; I just follow them."

"But, ReShonda, why do you have to take a pay cut?"

"Mother, I have to do this. I have to take a pay cut and then work my way back up. It's called paying dues."

"Damn, that," she replied. "Who's gonna pay your rent?"

That was the gist of my conversations whenever I wanted to do something my mother didn't agree with. But ten years later, as I'm back in Houston, working on-air for a television station, enjoying a nice salary and reflecting that it was all worth it, I still can't get my mother to admit that in that situation, she didn't know best.

"I always knew you'd make it. I just was worried about my baby, that's all," she now responds.

Part of deciphering when mother knows best is to know when to follow your heart. Something thirty-three-year-old Suzanne says she wishes she had done.

"I wanted to be an actress so bad. But I let my mother convince me to choose a more stable career as a teacher. I hate it with a passion and always wonder would I have made it in Hollywood had I followed my dream,"

Suzanne says. "If I could turn back time, I would follow my heart, not my mother's advice. Even if I had failed, at least I would have tried."

I TOLD YOU SO

You know those mothers who try to tell you something, you don't listen and they simply bite their tongues when things turn out just like they said? My mother isn't one of them. My mother's favorite words are "I told you so." That's usually followed by "You go'n learn to listen to your mother."

Single mother of three, Kenyatta knows that scenario all too well.

"My mother is the 'I told you so' Queen. She never hesitates to give her opinion. And Heaven forbid she should turn out to be right. You will hear 'I told you so' for days on end," Kenyatta says.

Forty-two-year-old Camille says she believes mothers don't get enough credit.

"While they may not always know what's best, a lot of times, they've been where we are," Camille says.

Roughly sixty-two percent of the women surveyed for this book say they have to give credit where credit is due. And that means admitting to their mothers that they wish they had listened to some important nugget of advice.

"For me, it was the credit cards," says twenty-nine-year-old Michelle. "My mother warned me before I went to college not to get them. But since they were giving them out to anyone with a student ID, I threw her advice to the wind. By the time I was a senior, I had nine credit cards. Needless to say since I didn't have a job, I couldn't pay the bills. Now, my credit score is so low, even the second-chance creditors turn me down. Man, I wish I had listened to my mother, who by the way has perfect credit."

"I didn't listen either," adds thirty-one-year-old Nikki. "My mother warned me not to get pregnant trying to hold onto a man. She said she had done it and it didn't do anything but hurt me and her. She wanted me to go down a different path. But for some reason, I didn't listen and did the exact same thing. And now, I see the only one hurting is me and my son. And my mother because she wasn't able to keep me from following in her footsteps."

FOLLOWING A DIFFERENT PATH

Jackie, a computer engineer, recalls a discussion she had with a white girl-friend. The girlfriend's mother constantly pushed her to "liberate herself." It's a concept Jackie didn't understand.

"My best friend in college, Heather, said her mother was constantly trying to get her to liberate herself. Break free from society's expectations and pursue a career. Heather's mom didn't work and she felt joy in seeing her daughter focus on her career. She called it liberation. I called it reality," Jackie says.

Women's studies professor Dr. Ruth Perry says what may have been liberation for white middle-class women in the mid-'70s, (i.e. getting out of their houses and going to work) was not necessarily liberation for black women who have usually worked outside the home and been responsible for taking care of their families as well. For some black women, liberation may well be the luxury of staying home and raising their children peacefully, rather than having to always balance work, household duties, childrearing, self-education, etcetera.

Dr. Perry describes this example.

"Several years ago I was teaching an 'Introduction to Women's Studies' class to a small group of seniors—a couple of black women and four white women. At a certain point in a discussion of black and white identity formation, we got on mother-daughter relationships. The black women in this class and one of the white women adored their mothers. The other white women were quite ambivalent. The white woman who adored her mother came from an all-female household. Her mother had several daughters by different men but she had never married, and was the sole supporter of her family. That was true of the black women as well.

"We theorized, on the basis of what the ambivalent students were saying, that their ambivalence was due to the message they got from their mothers about accommodating to male domination within a family setting. The women whose mothers did not have to accommodate to male authority were the ones who unambivalently respected their mothers. They understood that their mothers worked very hard to put bread on the table and to raise them, and they respected and admired them. Those women who watched their mothers accommodating to male power felt ambivalent about their mothers' lessons about what it meant to be an adult woman.

"We did a totally unstatistical, methodologically imperfect study, asking everybody we knew how they felt about their mothers. It seemed to corroborate our conclusions that family configurations in black families set a different kind of standard when the maternal head of household who is the breadwinner is not in a subordinate relation to a particular man.

"The messages she gives her daughter are not ambivalent about what it means to be in the world as an adult woman."

Dr. Perry is hesitant to generalize those ethnic differences beyond these people in her classroom, but says the study provided profound insight.

Jackie says it doesn't take an advanced degree or professional insight for her to see that Dr. Perry was right on target.

"My mother has always worked. Her mother worked. So liberating yourself by choosing to work is foreign to me. I guess that's simply because it's never been an option. It's funny though. Both my mom and Heather's mom wanted us to follow different paths than they did. (My mom did domestic labor.) And while the end destination was different, the prevailing factor was they wanted us to live a better life than they did."

REFLECTIONS

- ❦ Do you have a "Mother knows best" mom?
- ❦ What advice did your mother give you that you now wish you had listened to?
- ❦ Have you repeated any of your mother's mistakes? If so, what?

PART II

It's not so bad being like Mama

Chapter Four *Guilt trippin'*

"If I don't do whatever my mother asks me to do, I have to hear how she
was in labor with me for twenty-seven hours and didn't complain once."
                                                            —LYDIA, *twenty-five*

For my mother, watching the news is a daily ritual. And it usually never
fails. She'll call me after a story airs.

"ReShonda, it's your mother," she'll say as if my Caller ID and her voice
can't tell me.

"Hello, Mother. How are you today?"

"My carpel tunnel is acting up and I wish I could win the Lotto. But I'm
alive so I guess that counts for something. Are you watching the news?"

"I work in the news business, Mother."

"So then you saw the story about the woman who locked her children in
the closet."

"Yes, I know all about it."

"Mmm-hmmm, you should be grateful to have a mother like me who never
locked you in the closet."

Huh?

Or this repeated conversation:

"ReShonda, it's your mother. Did I sleep with you last night?"

"Excuse me," I responded.

"I'm just wondering if I slept with you last night since you didn't call me
today."

Long sigh.

"Mother, I talked with you yesterday."

"So what? I could've died overnight. I had a coughing fit and I couldn't breathe. I just knew that was it for me. And you wouldn't have even known until this evening because you hadn't bothered to call me. My body would've decomposed before you or your sister even checked on me. You saw that lady on the news last night. She was in her apartment dead for three days before anybody found her."

Another long sigh.

Eventually I just stopped trying to make sense of my mother's ability to find some way to incorporate current events into a reason why I should "thank God for my mama." I just came to realize Mom was guilt trippin'. For some reason she felt like she needed to lay a guilt trip on me so that I could appreciate her more. My mother could squeeze guilt from something as simple as a visit ("You need to be thankful you have a mother on top of this soil to visit," she'll say) or chauffeuring her around ("There are kids in Africa who wish they had a nice car like this to drive their mother around in.")

My sister, Tanisha, on the other hand, thinks my mom takes the guilt thing to another level by playing favorites.

"If I had a dime for every time Mama told me ReShonda is her favorite daughter, I'd be a rich woman. It usually comes right after I failed to take her call, take her to dinner, or something else that she wants me to do. The thing is, I know she doesn't really mean it; she just likes to try to make me feel guilty," Tanisha says.

My girlfriend Jaimi, however, believes her late mother had the guilt market cornered.

"My mother would ask me to do things for her and if I even remotely acted like I didn't want to, I'd get the whole, 'I can't believe you would tell your mother no' soliloquy. Then I would have to hear the whole story of how she sacrificed for me; how she went without just so I could have clothes on my back. The tirade would go on for twenty minutes. All because I didn't feel like taking her to the mall," Jaimi says.

"I think my mother is the queen of guilt," adds twenty-five-year-old Lydia. "If I disagree with her about anything; tell her no about anything, I have to hear how she was in labor with me for twenty-seven hours and how she almost died trying to bring me in the world."

Therapist and author Dr. Victoria Sloan says many mothers lay a guilt trip for a number of reasons, but most often to exert some sense of control.

"The reasons may vary from one mother to the next. One mother may use a guilt trip as a way to maintain an unhealthy degree of control over her child and that child becomes an adult and tries to make various decisions in their lives. Some other mothers may use guilt tripping because their daughter is achieving success they could only dream about. I've worked with quite a few mothers who were not the *Brady Bunch* typical sitcom moms; they had a lot of unresolved issues of their own. I've seen it happen quite a bit and it's very sad. But ultimately if a mother uses guilt as a way of trying to control or manipulate or influence a child and this is a consistent tool that they use, then what it says to me is that there is a serious communication problem between mother and daughter. And there needs to be some clearing of the air where they can speak honestly to one another about their feelings because ultimately guilt is a way to manipulate other people."

Forty-nine-year-old Doris says her mother's guilt trip is a reflection of their relationship.

"My mother is always complaining that I give my daughter more attention than my boys. But that's only because she feels guilty that she and I don't have the same kind of relationship as my daughter," Doris says.

Dr. Sloan says it is important to set boundaries, especially in those relationships where mothers use guilt as a tool to manipulate the relationship.

"Boundaries could be one of the most important things you have in a mother/daughter relationship. There has to be a mutual respect on each side. Both women have to see the other person as an adult who has the right to make her own choices, who has a mind to make her own thoughts. In the healthiest of relationships we give one another the freedom to disagree and we allow people to make their own decisions. Boundaries are important because the mother/daughter relationship really does change. It starts out on one level with mom having all the power and the child having none. Then as the child grows up and becomes a woman herself, now she and mom have to learn how to share and negotiate the power. Mom has to understand that her daughter is an adult now and she must be allowed to make her own choices. Years later, as the mom becomes elderly, then there is a role reversal so that now the daughter is in the care-taking role. It really goes full circle and evolves into so many things at so many times, there's a constant adjustment that has to go into a relationship."

It's advice forty-year-old Stephanie says she'll definitely use.

"I think that's what I need with my mom—boundaries. Whenever she comes to visit, I end up frustrated because she always intrudes on my way of doing things. She comes in, moves my furniture around, repositions my dishes and refolds my towels. It drives me insane. Maybe if I could set some boundaries, our visits would be much more pleasant," Stephanie says.

REFLECTIONS

❦ Is your mother guilty of guilt trippin'?

❦ Do you believe your mother's guilt trips are good-natured, harmless taunting, or tools of manipulation?

❦ What, if any, boundaries have you had to assess in your relationship with your mother?

CHAPTER FIVE

Passing it on

"My white friends would say things to their mom like, 'You're not my friend.' I tried it—once. My mom popped me in the mouth and then said, 'I don't want to be your friend, I'm your mama.'"

—MICHELLE, *thirty-five*

I t is an image that still haunts me. Me in my cheerleader uniform at the club after the big game (hey, it was the thing to do back then.) We had just beaten our rival high school football team and everyone was in a good mood. I felt on top of the world. Yeah, I knew it was past my eleven o'clock curfew, but I was having such a good time, I didn't care. I turned to my friend Kelli and said, "Screw it. I know my mom will be mad, but a couple of days on phone punishment won't kill me. It'll be worth it for all the fun I'm having."

I continued jamming with my friends. We were all on the dance floor doing the Cabbage Patch dance and just having a really good time. The party was jumping to the sounds of MC Hammer. Then suddenly the music just stopped. All eyes turned to the deejay, who leaned into the microphone and said, "Sorry to interrupt your groove, folks, but I've got an important message for one of our party-goers. ReShonda Tate, the Madison High School cheerleader, yo' mama is waiting for you outside in her pink hair rollers and boy is she pissed! She said for you to bring your fast behind on!"

Everyone slowly turned toward me. I stood in the middle of the dance floor, frozen in my dance position in my blue cheerleading uniform, utterly astonished. I wanted to die right there in the middle of the club. The laughing deejay interrupted my thoughts.

"Girl, you'd better get your ass on outside 'cause yo' mama look like she don't play!" The club erupted in laughter as he started the music back up. Unable to hold back the tears, I burst through the crowd and out the front door.

My mother was standing there with yes, her pink rollers (they were under a scarf, but you could see the rollers nonetheless.) Thankfully, she had on regular clothes and not a housecoat or something as I initially feared. Since it was almost two in the morning, I expected to see fury written across her face. Instead she stood there with a smirk.

"I guess you thought I was playing when I told you to have your little fast tail home by eleven?" she said.

Still too stunned to talk, I just stared at her. I wanted to scream, "How could you do this to me? How could you embarrass me in front of all my friends? I hate you!" I wanted to yell all that and more, but if your mother is anything like mine, then you'll understand that I could think whatever I wanted as long as I didn't ever dare say it.

"I ought to go upside your head right outside this club," my mother snapped, the smirk leaving her face. "I have been at home worried sick. The game was over at nine. It's almost two in the morning. I had to call Kelli's mother to find out where you were."

My mother rambled on as several people stood outside the club snickering. I ended up tuning my mother out so I don't really know what else she said. All I could think was that she had come to the club in her rollers.

Perhaps my mother knew that coming up to the club that night would be far worse punishment than taking away phone privileges. I don't know, but I swore I would never, ever do something like that to my child.

Fast forward twenty years. I was keeping my fifteen-year-old niece for the summer. We went out of town to a wedding and she decided she would sneak out of the hotel and stay out until five in the morning. I had no idea where she was. I called my mother hysterical. Despite the sleepiness in her voice, I could feel her smile through the phone.

"Umm-hmmm," she said. "You don't know if she's dead or alive, huh?"

"No," I cried. "She wasn't supposed to leave the hotel. It's four-thirty in the morning."

"Umm-hmmm," my mother responded. "Have you gotten ready for bed yet?"

"Huh?" I responded. "What does that have to do with anything?"

"I'm just asking," my mother calmly replied. "Have you rolled your hair yet?"

"My hair? Yes, but what does that have to do with anything?"

"If you knew where she was, what would you do?"

"I would go get her little behind right now!"

"Umm-hmmm. Hair rollers and all, right?"

"Of course. I wouldn't care about any hair rollers. I would just want to make sure she's safe and..." I stopped and smiled as I realized where my mother was going with this.

"That's just your niece. By marriage. Imagine if it was your daughter, the girl you brought into this world," my mother coolly replied.

I could only nod because she was absolutely right. It had taken twenty years, but finally I understood.

LIKE MOTHER, LIKE DAUGHTER

My friends like to tell me I'm a drama queen. Not to the extent that I like to have some madness going on in my life, but in the sense that I am simply dramatic in everything that I do. My mother says I've been that way since I was little girl. Like the time when I was eight and we were at a family gathering. I was lying down on my father's lap. After about twenty minutes, he got up to go somewhere and I couldn't lift my head.

I remember he started to panic. "Baby, baby, sit up," he frantically said as he tried to maneuver my limp body.

"Ummm," I just moaned as my eyes rolled in the back of my head.

Every time he tried to lift my head, I made these guttural elephant sounds. By this point, my mom and all my other relatives were freaking out. They decided to get me to the nearest hospital (this was a small town in Arkansas), which was about twenty minutes away. It was pouring down raining. My dad was carrying my limp body (my head was still flopped to the side) and their only goal was to get me to the hospital.

Halfway there, the car broke down. My parents jumped out of the car, lifted me out of the back seat and began walking in the rain. They managed to quickly flag down someone who graciously took us to the hospital.

Once there, the town doctor performed a thorough examination. My parents waited with baited breath. Once he finished his examination, Dr. Warren turned toward my parents.

"What's wrong with her?" my father nervously asked.

Dr. Warren smiled. "Nothing that a little attention can't cure."

"Attention?" my mother asked, confused.

"Yep," Dr. Warren replied. "ReShonda." He tapped me on the shoulder. I moaned but didn't move. "Sit up, gal."

Still I didn't budge.

He put a little more force in his voice. "I said, sit up, gal." I knew Dr. Warren didn't play, so I eased up, a small smile across my face.

"I tricked you," I softly said, hoping my parents saw the humor.

Needless to say, my parents were livid, especially my mother.

My Grandma Pearly saved me from God only knows what that day as my mother was beyond furious. Grandma had met us at the hospital and like me, she found the whole incident rather amusing. It took her reminding my mother about the time my mom wanted to go on a trip with them (my grandparents) and was told she had to stay at home. My mother hid in the back seat of their car, clad only in her underwear. By the time my grandparents discovered her, they were near their destination, some ninety miles away. They then had to drive around for hours to find my mother some clothes. All my mother could do was smile. So Grandma used to always say I came by my theatrics honestly.

Perhaps that's why it shouldn't surprise me that my daughter had a panic attack when I told her I was calling Santa Claus because she wouldn't mind; or that she put on seven layers of clothing the day she knew she was going to get a spanking when I got home; or even when, at four, she fell on the floor and said she "was going to meet her maker" after bumping her head. Nope, none of her drama-filled antics should surprise me. Because a quick perusal of my family tree gives credence to the phrase, "like mother, like daughter."

Drama is something twenty-eight-year-old Alexis knows all too well. But her drama *is* the kind that does entail constant madness.

"It's something in our genes," Alexis laughed. "My grandmother acted a fool with my grandfather. He talked to her the wrong way, called her out her name one time too many, and she busted him upside his head with a horseshoe. Years later, my mother stabbed my father with some sewing shears after they got into an argument and he hit her. I'm almost scared to get married because I know the penchant for drama is in my blood. Try as I may, I can't stop acting a fool with my boyfriend when he makes me mad. While I haven't tried to stab him or hit him upside the head yet, I definitely can't promise that it would never happen. Unfortunately, I inherited my mother's volatile temper, and she got it from her mother. Good Lord, how do we make it stop?"

BREAKING THE CYCLE

Forty-four-year-old Sandy says she too has broken those childhood promises not to raise her children like she was raised.

"My mother was so strict," Sandy says. "Growing up, I used to think she was unbelievably strict. Now, that my daughter just turned sixteen, I think I'm worse than my mom."

"She is," Sandy's daughter, Kyla, chimed in. "I feel like a prisoner."

"In this day and age, you have to be strict. It's too many psychos out there," Sandy says.

Michelle says she also rears her children differently than she was reared.

"I saw way too much growing up. I don't hide things from my son. When topics come up I am always willing to discuss them, even graphically. However, the things I witnessed from my mom as a child my son will NEVER see in me," Michelle says.

Thirty-seven-year-old Angela admits she raises her children differently from her mother, but she says she does exhibit some characteristics of her mother in the child-rearing process.

"It's a little thing, but I used to think my mother was crazy because she followed us around the house turning off lights. She would complain and fuss constantly if we left the TV on and no one was watching it; or if we pushed the thermostat down to sixty degrees; or if we stood in the refrigerator trying to decide what we would eat. It wasn't until I got a family of my own—and my first light bill—that I understood," Angela says. "Now I follow my kids around the house turning off lights."

"My quirky trait is lightning," added forty-year-old Shawnee. "My mother used to make us turn off all the TVs, radios, and any other electrical appliance any time it was lightning. We couldn't even play. We just had to sit there until it stopped lightning. I used to think it was absurd. Now, I find myself doing the same thing with my kids."

"I wish there was some magic pill that I could take that would wipe out all the negative things I picked up from my mother," says twenty-one-year-old Evelyn.

If only it were that easy. If it were, many of us would just turn off those negative traits and live happily ever after. But just like we accept the good things, we have to accept the bad. But change can happen, Dr. Victoria Sloan says.

"Breaking destructive cycles takes hard work and determination," she says.

Dr. Sloan, author of *Dancing with Destiny*, says it is important not to beat yourself up when you find yourself following in your mother's footsteps.

Many of the women interviewed say they see the way they were treated as part of a cycle. For Julie, she watched as her grandmother treated her mother badly, a trait Julie's mother now passes on to her.

"A lot of her anger comes from the way her mom treated her and the lack of attention she received as a child from her. To this day, her mom only calls her when she needs something, and my mom does me the same way," says Julie.

And for many, it takes steadfast determination to break the cycle.

"If I wasn't strongwilled and determined to not be like the other women in my family, I probably would have a child out of wedlock by now and no college education. I recognized the things about them I didn't like, and I continued to strive to be different," says thirty-year-old ShaRonda.

It's just the opposite for Tonya. She says her childrearing is a direct reflection of how her mother raised her.

"She spent a lot of time intentionally exposing me to various cultures, cities, people, and I try to do the same with my kids. Also, I do try to emphasize to my kids that it is imperative to treat people kindly no matter how bad they treat you and always, always forgive. It takes too much energy to hate and I learned that from my mother," Tonya says.

REFLECTIONS

❦ What is something your mother did while you were growing up that you swore you would never do?

❦ If you have children, do you find yourself doing any of those things?

❦ Is there anything about your mother that you have to conscientiously work at to keep from emulating?

CHAPTER SIX *Lovin' like Mama*

*"My mother has been married four times. I'm sticking it out in a marriage
I know is no good because I don't want to end up like that."*

—SHARON, *thirty-nine*

Sit down with your grandmother and she'll probably tell you how back
in her day, women stuck with their husbands—no matter what.

Twenty-six-year-old Eva remembers her grandmother sitting by the old
wood stove in their small, three-bedroom home, waiting well into the night
for her husband to come home.

"Mudear would just sit there, rocking back and forth, anger etched across
her face. Pawpaw would come in around three or four, reeking of another
woman's scent. Mudear would just shoot him an evil look—then go to bed,"
Eva says. "Back then, women didn't leave. They dealt with it all, abuse,
infidelity, you name it. They had a 'boys will be boys' mentality."

However, the rules changed when it came to Eva's mother.

"The first time my mother caught my father having an affair, she left,"
Carolyn adds.

As divorce became more acceptable, many women in the baby boomer
generation were quick to develop the mantra, "I can do bad all by myself."
Gone was the forgiving nature of their mothers, the ability to put on visors
and be oblivious to infidelity. And while many still harbored the "boys will
be boys" mentality, more and more women began to tell themselves they
didn't have to accept just anything from a man.

Shirley, a twenty-four-year-old teacher, gives this example: "My mother put up with a lot from my father. She forgave him for a couple of affairs. Then, I think she just reached a point where she said, 'Forget this. I can do this by myself and not have to put up with less than I deserve.'"

Part of the ability to develop that attitude and walk away comes from financial status. According to the 2002 U.S. Census, in minority two-parent households, 94 percent of the women work.

"I think that's why my mom left," Shirley adds. "She felt like she could support us on her own. She didn't need to stay with my father in order to make ends meet. She could meet them herself. And although it was hard, she did it."

But Shirley is quick to add that independence can sometimes backfire.

"My marriage lasted seven months. I think I was like my mother in that I didn't want to deal with anything less than what I felt I deserved. So instead of sticking it out, trying to make it work, I left. I figured I had my own money and I didn't need him. It's a decision I regret now because marriage is about work, and I never gave it a shot. And now, he has his act together and is happily married to someone else."

Fifty-three-year-old Jeanine says if she didn't teach her daughter anything else, she taught her to accept only the best from a man.

"I'm a strong woman. My daughter and I have battled since she was thirteen years old, but it was worth it if I can get her to recognize her strength as well," Jeanine says.

Jeanine's daughter, Kristie, says her mother's efforts were not in vain.

"That is one area where I'm glad I took after my mother. I'm not going to waste my time on a man who's not giving me what I deserve," Kristie says. "When I was growing up, my mom stayed single rather than deal with a trifling man. I couldn't understand it then. But now, not only do I understand it, I respect it."

It's a philosophy thirty-one-year-old Roxanne wishes her mother had adopted.

"My mother was one of those who stayed. She felt having a piece of man was better than no man at all," says Roxanne. "And it made me sick to my stomach. I was determined to be independent enough that I would never have to endure that."

It's that independence that Roxanne now believes is keeping her from finding a mate.

"I think I'm too independent, too strong-minded. If my mother had been strong enough to leave and not subject my sister and me to her weaknesses, maybe my views on dealing with men would be different, and I'd have the husband and two kids I've always dreamed of."

For thirty-nine-year-old Sharon, it's about *not* following in her mother's footsteps. She readily admits she's in an unhappy marriage. Her husband doesn't cheat (to her knowledge, she adds), and he's a good provider. But she and her husband have absolutely nothing in common.

"We are totally incompatible. He's a dreamer. I'm a doer. He's a homebody. I'm a socialite. We're definitely not meant for each other," Sharon says.

So why does she stay?

"My mother," Sharon responds matter-of-factly. "She had me when she was seventeen. She never married my father and has been married four times to different men since then. So when I turned up pregnant at eighteen, I freaked. I jumped into marriage with my husband and I've held on from fear that I too would travel down that matrimonial road four times."

It was the same story for forty-nine-year-old Doris. "I found myself attracted to the same kind of men as my mother. I married a man just like the man she married even though I hated her husband and the things he did to her," she says.

Of the women interviewed for this book, sixty-nine percent say they don't approve of their mother's relationship with men. Most say their mothers definitely didn't lead by example when it came to lessons in love.

For example, twenty-nine-year-old Trina says the way her mother handled men has had a negative effect on her own relationships.

"When I was younger, I viewed my mother's emotional ways as weak. When my parents would argue, for example, my mother would cry. To this day, when I'm hurt, my first instinct is to strike back so I won't give someone else the satisfaction of knowing that they hurt me. I cry in private," she says.

For forty-two-year-old Evelyn, lovin' like Mama isn't a bad thing.

"My mother didn't take no stuff from her man, and neither do I."

But Evelyn's boyfriend, Rick, says it's that attitude that has kept them from the altar.

"Evelyn listens to all this hard-core stuff her mother spouts out, and it's going to make her end up a lonely, bitter, old woman—just like her mother. Her mom believes in having separate bank accounts, a man on the side, just in case, and other stuff like that. I see Evelyn emulating that. But what she doesn't realize is that bitterness has caused her mother to be like that. She's letting her mother's bitterness steal her joy," Rick says.

Feminist lecturer bell hooks says part of that attitude is rooted in history. In *Sisters of the Yam*, she says, "…women who learned to keep a bit of money stashed away somewhere that he (their husband) didn't know about, were responding to the reality of domestic cruelty and violence and the need to have means to escape."

That attitude, hooks writes, did more harm than good. "The negative impact of these strategies was that truth-telling, honest and open communication was less and less seen as necessary to the building of positive relationships."

If your mother is anything like mine, she won't hesitate to give you her two cents on love. Don't discount it all. But make sure you look at the bigger picture. As wise as our mothers are, you must remember, they are women too, with loving hearts—hearts that if broken, can change their views of love.

My mother is one of those who gave her heart to men—only to have it crushed. And now, like Evelyn's mother, it has made her bitter. She's not one of those "all men are dogs" moms (more on that later), but she is definitely not pro-love.

"I used to be," my mother is quick to say. "But not anymore. When you've traveled down the road that I have, you just don't have it in you anymore."

One of the phrases she loves spouting to me is, "just keep living." She's sure, sooner or later, I'll come around to her way of thinking.

"My mother tried to tell me and I wouldn't listen. So just keep living and you'll see for yourself," she says.

Maybe I will. But as for now, I can't let her pain hurt my relationships. I can just hear my mother as she's reading this. "Don't be a fool all your life," she's most likely muttering. But what my mother, and many others like her, don't realize is, she didn't raise a fool for a daughter. Just because we choose to not let their lives determine how we'll live ours, doesn't mean we aren't prepared when life throws us curves. If my mate cheats, then it's his loss. Yes, I'll be hurt, but I'll heal. We have to raise our daughters with that mentality so that when a good man does come their way, they don't let negativity ruin their chance at happiness. Keep in mind, harboring a negative attitude regarding men is injected into our sons, who feel they're only living up to the expectations of the women in their lives.

"DON'T TRUST HIM AS FAR AS YOU CAN SEE HIM."

Mothers have a natural instinct to want to protect us from pain. Many will tell you it's the basis for all of their actions. They just don't want to see you go through what they did. But it's important to recognize that their life is not your life. The man who cheated on them is not your man. The man who treated them with disrespect is not your man. Buying into your mother's train of thought that men in general are no good will cause you to go into a relationship with negative feelings.

That's exactly what happened to thirty-five-year-old Shawn.

"That's all I've heard all my life," Shawn says. "Men are no good. It was my mother's national anthem. So I grew up believing it, even gravitating toward men who were known players—simply to have validation of what my mother told me all my life."

After a series of short-lived relationships, Shawn says she wishes she had set her own standards.

"As I look back on all my failed relationships, I can't help but wonder would they have turned out differently if I hadn't been fed such negativity growing up," she says.

While many mothers would argue they simply have a more realistic view of men, we have to learn to find a balance, taking in our mother's wisdom, but not letting our actions be a reaction of something that occurred in their lives.

REFLECTIONS

❦ Assess your mother's relationships with men. Do you find that yours is mirroring hers?

❦ Or in your quest NOT to follow in your mother's footsteps, do you find yourself suffering anyway?

❦ Is there an underlying reason behind your mother's motives when she offers up lessons in love?

❦ Are you letting your mother's experience with one man block your blessings from another?

CHAPTER SEVEN *Tellin' it like it is*

"My seven-year-old son came into my room recently and proudly boasted that he could imitate me. My heart warmed as I watched him clear his throat, take a deep breath like he was getting ready for a major performance and then as loud as he could yell, 'Sit down! Shut up! Do you hear me talking to you!' As he gallantly smiled, I was mortified. Not only because that was how my child saw me, but because that's just how I felt my mother used to sound to me."

—NINA, *thirty-nine*

My girlfriend Nina says that day was a revelation to her. She was hurt that the defining thing that stood out about her to her son was how she sounded.

"I mean it said a lot. He didn't think anything of it, but I'm glad he brought it to my attention. My mother used to holler at us all the time, and I remember wishing she would talk to us like somebody with some sense. I didn't realize I was doing the same thing until my son's 'imitation' of me," Nina says.

Twenty-eight-year-old Danielle says she too remembers an exorbitant amount of yelling going on in her house as she was growing up.

"I can't remember a single day when my mother wasn't yelling at me and my siblings about something," Danielle says.

And unfortunately, it's a pattern that has continued into her own home.

"As much as I hate to admit it, I find myself yelling at my kids all the time, too. And it's not just my children. My husband is constantly admonishing me to watch my tone. I swear I am my mother when it comes to the way we talk. People even say we sound just alike," she says. "It may be a little thing to some people, but it's a big deal to me."

But more than that, Danielle says she is most concerned that the communication traits she picked up from her mother run much deeper than simple conversation.

"I also communicate, or should I say don't communicate, just like she did. I watched her shut down when problems were bothering her. I watched how difficult a time she had trying to communicate her feelings to my father. It was a source of constant arguments for her. It's the same way for my husband and me," Danielle says. "We don't communicate and I know it's all my fault. It's another negative trait I picked up from my mother. But unlike her, I'm trying to work on it. Her failure to communicate led to her divorce from my father. I'm trying not to go down that same road."

Communication is perhaps one of the strongest traits we pick up from our mothers. Not just in how we communicate *to* others, but how we communicate *with* others. Whether it's how we communicate with our significant others, our children, or in our day-to-day relationships, our communication traits can most often be traced back to our mothers.

For Karen, the communication was not in what her mother said, but in what she *didn't* say. Karen remembers how her mother's inability to communicate her feelings hurt her as a child. She's determined not to do the same to her child.

"I tell my son every day that I love him and show him just by holding him, laughing with him, playing with him," she says.

And she doesn't let the negativity her mother spewed upon her growing up affect her relationship with her children.

"Although my son's father and I are not together, my son will never be told anything negative about him or how he is like him in a negative sense. I just won't go there," she says.

TELLIN' IT LIKE IT T-I-S

If I ever want to know the truth to a question like, "Do I look fat in this outfit?" or "Is my hair cute like this?" all I need to do is ask my mama.

I remember being proud of an exclusive news story I had reported on the nightly news. I anxiously called my mother, because again, I can count on her to "keep it real."

"Hey, Ma, did you catch my story tonight?" I asked her.

"Umm-huh," she replied.

"What did you think? I mean, it was a really powerful piece, edited well. I had to really work hard to get that story. I think it'll really touch some people's lives, don't you think?"

"I'm sure it will. But tell me this, why in the world would you wear that outfit on TV?"

"Excuse me?"

"It made you look twenty pounds heavier. You took up half my big screen. And what's wrong with your hair? I thought you went to the beauty shop yesterday?"

I could only smile. After all, that's my mama.

Sure, there are some mothers who will try to sugarcoat things to make you feel better, but my mother is not one of them.

She tells it like it is.

And I love her for it. Many of the women I talked to for this book feel the same way about their mothers telling it like it is.

"That straightforwardness keeps me on my toes," says my friend Angela, whose mother also doesn't spare any feelings. "I have some relatives who will always try to tell you what you want to hear. My mother has caught some flak from them because she is so real, but if you can't count on your mother to keep it real, who can you count on?"

But another friend, Dee, doesn't agree with that theory.

"I think that directness can backfire. It can be stifling. Mothers don't have to shoot down a child's dream by being brutally honest."

"That's crazy," responds thirty-year-old Dana. "I guess a mother should say, 'Baby, you sing so well' to a daughter who can't hold a note? Then the girl will go on *American Idol* and make a fool out of everybody."

Let's just be real; sometimes feelings will get hurt. That's where having thick skin comes in and knowing when the criticism is done out of love.

"The constructive criticism is only for your own good," says sixty-year-old

Peggy, mother of five girls. "Besides, we're only telling you what people will whisper behind your back. If my daughter is wearing something outlandish, or does something crazy, I'm going to tell her about it. Remember that which does not break you makes you stronger. And that's all us mothers are trying to do. Make our babies stronger."

REFLECTIONS

❧ What type of communicator would you say your mother was?

❧ Do your communication skills mirror those of your mother? If so, how? If not, how are they different?

❧ Is your mother more of a pacifier or does she shoot straight from the hip?

PART III

Movin' on

Chapter Eight *Mama drama*

"My mother is a cantankerous, part-time Christian, full-time Hell Raiser. She is conniving, untrustworthy and my mother. I love her, but I can't be with her or be like her."

—FRANCINE, *thirty-eight*

While more than seventy-five percent of the women surveyed for this book said their relationships with their mothers were either "outstanding" or "okay," several said the best relationship they can have with their mother is one where they never talk. Much of the dissension comes from "mama drama."

For Rochelle, it was a down payment on a home that was at the center of her problems with her mother. Rochelle says her mother offered the money as a gift—until they had an argument.

"Then she started talking about 'I need my money back,' which was ludicrous because the money was in our escrow account waiting on us to close," Rochelle says.

When Rochelle refused to return the money, her mother was livid.

"She turned into this vile human being who I didn't know," Rochelle says.

"I gave Ro and her husband the money because I came into some extra money and felt as a mother, it was my duty," her mother, Iris, says. "But I also had boundaries for how much the house they got should cost. She didn't include me on the search, didn't solicit my opinion, then when I finally saw the house, I was dumbfounded. They can't afford that house and I refuse to contribute to them getting themselves deeper in debt. Besides, I gave her the money out of a deep love that I no longer feel. She has acted so ugly throughout all of this that I don't even want to claim her as my daughter."

Syndicated advice columnist and author Harriette Cole says that Rochelle and Iris have reached a crossroads in their relationship that is normal for many adult mothers and daughters. The main challenge she says is to meet each other where they are now, in the moment. They have to let go of the hurts. What happened in the past has to stay in the past.

"They have all this history," says Cole. "Instead of dwelling on the past, they should try to focus on the future."

Rochelle and Iris have unresolved issues regarding money, which is a huge issue for many people.

"This is all about control," Rochelle says. "She's mad because I didn't let her control the kind of house I got. If the money was a gift then it's none of her business what I do with it."

Iris begs to differ.

"If you don't want my input, don't take my money. My problem with the house is that they can't afford it. If one of them loses their job, or worse yet, her husband bails out on her, I'm the one who will have to step in and pick up the pieces. Just like I've always done," Iris says.

"The problem is that it's not about the money, it's about the relationship," says Cole. "The money is just a symbol of something bigger."

Money was the root of Erica's problems with her mother, Jewel, who had Erica "hold" some money for her. When she asked for it back, Erica had spent it. Erica says she made arrangements with her mother to pay the money back in installments, but her mother wasn't hearing it.

"I understand she was mad, she had a right to be mad. But then she started talking real crazy to me and I just said forget it, I'll pay her back when I pay her back," Erica says.

Things got even worse when Jewel took her daughter to court to retrieve her money.

"I can't believe she would sue me over a funky couple of thousand dollars," Erica says.

Jewel lost the case because of the statue of limitations. She had waited too long to sue. But in the process she also lost her daughter.

"We will never be the same again," Jewel says. "As far as I'm concerned, my daughter is dead."

For Yvonne, every trip home to her mother ends in disaster. She says her mother's gossipy nature is at the root of her family's problems.

"My mother gets on my nerves talking about my siblings to me and then talking about me to them. Telling her to not go there only created a bigger gap in our not-so close relationship (right now we are going through one of our long silent sessions. She came for the Christmas holiday and wrecked shop and had to be sent back one month early). Burned bridges are hard to repair. I've done a lot of construction in our relationship," Yvonne says.

Drama is bound to happen in a relationship with two grown women–especially two strong-minded women. Then when you throw in a child who no longer wants to be treated like a child, but rather a woman within her own right, conflict is bound to arise, Dr. Victoria Sloan adds.

"The true test is in how you deal with it," she says.

REFLECTIONS

- ❧ Do you hold grudges that affect your relationship with your mother/daughter? If so, what are they?
- ❧ Does your mother totally accept your "womanhood?"
- ❧ What are some instances of "mama drama" you've had with your mother?

CHAPTER NINE *Mama did the best she could*

"When you're young you think what your mother tells you or does is crazy. But when you become a mother, it all becomes clear. She only wants the best for you."

—LaShaunda, *twenty-six*

Growing up, thirty-year-old Michelle complained constantly about what she called unfair treatment between her and her siblings.

"There are so many things that my mom did while raising us and while she's continuing to raise my brothers, that I disagree with. When I was a junior in high school my mother would say to me, "Be home by ten p.m. or don't come home. But my brothers, when they were fourteen and fifteen could stay out until all hours of the night," says Michelle.

Sixty-four-year-old Eunice says the reasoning is simple.

"My daughter, Kendra, thought I was mean to her because I was easier on her brothers than I was on her. She would always cry about how I wasn't being fair. What she doesn't understand is that we live in a society that isn't fair. While I don't condone my sons being whoremongers, as my grandmother used to say, society is much more accepting of them being promiscuous than her, so I buckled down tighter on her," Eunice says.

Dr. Victoria Sloan says it is imperative that we understand that our mothers did the best they could.

"We have to understand this not just intellectually, but in the depths of our soul, where for some of us, their fallings left silent scars," Dr. Sloan says.

Sloan, who has counseled hundreds of women, says we must also remember that oftentimes our mothers are only giving us an extension of what their mothers gave them.

"We must remember that too many of our mothers were hurt by what their own mothers failed to give them," Dr. Sloan says. "But not because our grandmothers wanted to deny their daughters. Rather they also may have been unable to perceive, let alone respond to, their daughters' needs. In many families, it is a chain of unexpressed heartache that can reach back for generations."

Despite what many of us grew up believing, the fact is that our mothers are not perfect. Even under the most ideal circumstances, they are human and fallible beings who generally want the best for us, but need our input to understand how they can best support us.

Counselors also argue that daughters need to make the effort to learn how we can nurture our mothers in return. We may find that mothers are as in need of our support as we are of theirs. When they become mothers themselves, many women discover how deeply their own mothers really did love them, and how fervent a mother's need for her daughter's unconditional love can be.

But no matter what your relationship is with your mother, there comes a point when you must set boundaries. Your mother may never develop the self-confidence that will let her respect your point of views. That's why it's critical that you focus on yourself and not look to her to change. Your sense of self-worth will never improve if you keep letting her treat you in ways that you disagree with.

According to the Mayo Clinic Women's *HealthSource*, the crucial mother-daughter relationship changes as both age, and there are several ways to improve it along the way. Karen Fingerman, Ph.D, author of *Aging Mothers and Their Adult Daughters: A Study of Mixed Emotions*, says mother-daughter relationships take on different characteristics at different stages of life.

"When daughters become young adults, the focus of the mother-daughter relationship is the daughter's efforts to become an adult," Fingerman says.

While this is rewarding for the mother, Fingerman says it is also a significant expenditure of time and energy that focuses on one person—the daughter.

As daughters move into middle age and mothers grow older, their goals are more in sync. They have a mutual and more mature relationship with shared concerns. Dr. Fingerman recommends acceptance above all else as the key to improving relationships and avoiding crises.

"The best mother-daughter ties are ones where they care so much they see the other's faults but want to protect the other from knowing that they see them," she says.

California psychologist and mother-advocate Charney Herst believes both daughters and mothers must accept responsibility for the rifts that rock the mother-daughter bond.

In *For Mothers of Difficult Daughters—How to Enrich and Repair the Relationship in Adulthood,* she describes three archetypal "difficult daughters"—distant, dissatisfied and dependent. Herst still refuses to cast blame.

"There are bad mothers who abandon and abuse, but look at all the good mothers who devote all their time to mothering," she says.

Herst maintains that it doesn't matter what kind of relationship you have, as long as you have one.

"The relationship you have with your mother-daughter is one you create, by who you are and what you want from each other. You have to negotiate, confront and mediate," she says.

REFLECTIONS

❦ What are some mutual goals that you share with your mother?

❦ How has your relationship with your mother evolved over the years?

CHAPTER TEN *Working it out*

"I am not where I want to be in life, professionally or personally. I think it's because I harbor so much hatred for my mother, who was on drugs. People say it's time for me to forgive my mother so I can move on. If only it were that easy."
—KIM, *twenty-seven*

Kim vividly remembers the first thing her mother ever taught her.

"She taught me how to roll a joint. Three years old and I could roll a joint better than half the adults I knew," she says.

It's nothing she's by any means proud of. In fact, Kim says the memory makes her sick.

"My mother was a bona fide addict, who neglected everything and everybody in search of her next high. I don't remember trips to the park, frolicking around in the backyard, Christmas, birthdays, nothing. Just the weed, then the crack," Kim says.

Kim's mother died of a drug overdose when Kim was twenty-five. She says she had mixed emotions about her death.

"I went to the funeral, but I couldn't even cry. All I felt was hate. Hate and relief that she was gone," Kim says.

Kim has flitted about from job to job. She can't keep a man, doesn't even know if she wants to. And she blames her position in life on her mother.

"I'm not on drugs; in fact I despise them, but how am I supposed to be a productive member of society when I have so much bitterness toward the way I was raised?" she asked. "I missed so much of my past, that I have no hope for my future."

Dr. Sloan says the first thing Kim needs to do is forgive her mother, releasing those chains from the past.

"Those chains will wear you down if you don't let them go. You will go through all stages of healing but you can reach forgiveness. Unresolved issues are the root of many problems," she says.

But for people like forty-one-year-old Denise, forgiveness is not an option.

"My mother is the most insensitive, cruel human being I have ever known. I know that those words may seem mean, but I mean them from the depths of my soul. She allowed my stepfather to sexually and mentally abuse me for many years and did nothing about it," Denise says.

Dr. Sloan says an inability to forgive can affect all of your relationships, even those with other women.

"We tend to shift our issues with our mothers to all women because we haven't dealt with those toxic issues with our mothers. Our relationships with our mother prepare us to deal with issues of the world. If we don't have a healthy relationship, then the seeds we plant will grow very toxic," Dr. Sloan says. "It sets the stage to have lifelong problems, especially with women and sets unrealistic expectations with men. You can find yourself hating all women and having very few women friends."

In order to work through that, Dr. Sloan says there are a number of things you must do.

"Go to the source. What didn't your mother do? Did she not protect you? Did she fall short in showing you love? It's about you and your mother and until you deal with those issues, you'll displace them on all women."

That's exactly what twenty-six-year-old Donna believes happened to her.

"I've always wondered why I had a hard time keeping women friends, but I guess that's it. My mother was so conniving and selfish. I watched her backstab not only her friends, but family members as well. To this day, I don't trust women," Donna says.

"Our relationships with our mothers are like prescription lens glasses," Dr. Sloan adds. "They're coloring our entire experience with the world, and our vision of the world is off. We don't understand how or why. Therapy can help focus."

Dr. Sloan says therapy can also help you recognize destructive cycles.

"You have to own that this is an inter-generational problem within family lines. In order to break the cycle, you have to first acknowledge that there's a problem. You have to understand how that cycle affects each and every member of the family, and you have to do whatever it takes to find a way of breaking the cycle. If not, it will most definitely continue. The only thing you have to do is look back at all the previous generations who have suffered from the same type of conflicts and issues."

Dr. Sloan suggests making a genogram to help you work through those issues.

"That's where you map out generational and family history. That's a real powerful thing for people to see. The presence of problems, addictions, issues, struggles across the family lines. Sit down and draw out your family and chart out your mother, father and children. Look at all the addictions and discuss behavior patterns and more often than not, many of the problems your mom had, her mom had. You can really see how illnesses have permeated all of the generations."

In the past, many people, especially those in the African-American community, wouldn't seek therapy.

"When I started in 1985, about eighty percent of my clients were white. About five percent were black. Now, in 2005, ninety percent of my clients are African American. What I am seeing as a therapist over the course of my career is we have more African-American ministers who are of this generation. They are not old school in the sense of 'tell God your problems, not a shrink.' You have a more educated group of ministers who realize that some people need serious help, and that it is not in conflict with their beliefs about God and His healing power for them to go out and get therapy. We have more ministers and people in general, who are actually endorsing psychotherapy and getting help from the pulpit than we had prior to the '80s. People are getting a different message these days," Sloan says.

Let's face it, not every mother will respond to the "professional" way of healing or bettering their relationships.

"My mother would be highly insulted if I even talked about seeing a therapist. Not only would she not like me telling a complete stranger our business, but she feels therapy is for 'uppity folks.' We probably need it more than anyone else, but there's no way in hell my mother would ever go," Donna says.

Some, like Nina's mother, would act a downright fool.

"Tell that psycho babble to somebody whose mama ain't crazy. Because mine sure is." Nina laughed. "I tried the whole 'therapy' thing trying to work through things with my mother because we have a very strained relationship. First of all, she refused to go with me. Then when I tried to implement some of the things I learned in therapy to try and strengthen our relationship, she told me to take that dime-store diagnosis to the 'white folks.' I can only throw my hands up and accept that that is just the way my mother is. Our relationship will never be productive; it will never change because I don't think she's capable of change."

In these situations, Dr. Sloan says the daughter should simply continue to seek therapy, work on herself and learn how to better deal with her mother.

MOVING FORWARD

Regardless of whether the pain was intentional, it is imperative that we forgive our mothers for hurting us. Many women who are unable to cross that bridge of forgiveness know that something within them remains unsatisfied. And many feel getting satisfaction can only come from their mothers.

This is particularly true in households where fathers were often absent and the world beyond the front door can be dangerous and hostile. Now that we are grown and more able to speak up, a resentful silence has become a habit for some of us. Sometimes the bond has strengthened. Other times we may have been so blunted and embittered by our psychological injuries that we do little to bring about the understanding that might truly heal our relationships.

Forgiving our parents is a core task of adulthood, and one of the most crucial kinds of forgiveness. We see our parents in our mates, in our friends, in our bosses, even in our children. When we've felt rejected by a parent and have remained in that state, we will inevitably feel rejected by these important others as well.

"Forgiveness is the best thing I've ever done," says forty-year-old Tonja.

"My mother wasn't the best mother, and I nursed a lot of resentment from that. And I was unhappy for many years. But the minute I let that anger go; the minute I forgave my mother and focused on moving forward, my life changed for the better."

For those still struggling with their own personal mama dramas, you owe it to yourselves, to your children and to your mothers to heal the anger that keeps you stuck. The easiest way to accomplish this is through more open, honest communication. Start by telling your mother how she has hurt you and in a loving way, explain exactly how she can assist you in becoming the woman you desire to be.

EASIER SAID THAN DONE

For people like forty-one year old Denise, forgiveness is not an option.

"My mother is the most insensitive, cruel human being I have ever known. I know that these words may seem harsh, but I mean them from the depths of my soul. She allowed my stepfather to sexually and mentally abuse me for many years and did nothing about it," Denise says.

Although Sheryl's relationship with her mother differs from Denise's, her anger is the same.

"My mother abandoned me and my siblings when we were still very young. My grandmother raised me, and it was a struggle beyond belief. My mother shows up twenty years later looking all spiffy and things, and expects us to forgive her and welcome her back with open arms. I don't think so. The sad part is people tell me I look, talk and act just like her. I'll never know because I'll never get that close to her to ever find out," Sheryl says.

NOBODY LIKE MY MAMA

Despite the negative stories shared by the girlfriends in this book, the vast majority said they had wonderful relationships with their mothers. Most were like me, who despite the ups and downs, wouldn't trade their mothers for anything in the world.

"It's just a special bond; I can't explain it," says twenty-eight-year-old Tamara. "I mean, I love my father to no end, but it's just something different about my relationship with my mother. I feel from the bottom of my heart that despite our differences, despite whatever I may do, her love is unconditional."

Psychologist Robert Karen says that type of happiness comes from acceptance—of the good and the bad about our mothers. He says letting our mothers off the hook is the first step toward happiness, self-acceptance and maturity. Karen argues that when your mother can't change, work on changing yourself.

Here are some thoughts to help the healing begin:

Resolve resentment

Nursing resentment toward your mother does more than keep her in the doghouse. You get stuck there, too. When we hold a grudge against our mothers, we are clinging not just to her, but more specifically to the bad part of her. It's as if we don't want to live our lives until we have this resolved and feel the security of their unconditional love. We do so for good reasons psychologically. But the result is just the opposite: We stay locked into the badness, forever focusing on the negative.

Develop realistic expectations

The sins of parents are among the most difficult to forgive. We expect the world of them, and we don't want to lower our expectations. Decade after decade, we hold out the hope, often unconsciously, that they will finally do right by us. We want them to own up to all their misdeeds, to apologize, to make heartfelt pleas for our forgiveness. We want our parents to embrace us, to tell us they know we are good children, to undo the favoritism they've shown to a brother or sister, to take back their hurtful criticisms, to give us their praise. Be prepared to deal with the "what ifs," i.e., what if that never happens.

Remember the good times

Most mothers love their children, with surprisingly few exceptions. But no parent is perfect, which means that everyone has childhood wounds. If we're lucky, our parents were good enough for us to be able to hold on to the knowledge of their love for us and our love for them, even in the face of the things they did that hurt us. Even if negativity clouds your memories, try to remember some of the good.

Grow up

To forgive is not to condone the bad things our parents have done. It's not to deny their selfishness, their rejections, their meanness, their brutality, or any of the other misdeeds, character flaws, or limitations that may attach to them. It is important that we separate from our parents and stop seeing ourselves as children who depend on them for our emotional well-being. Stop being their victims and recognize that you are an adult with some capacity to shape your own life, and in fact, have a responsibility to do so.

Let your mother back into your heart

When we do that, we can begin to understand the circumstances and limitations they labored under; recognize the goodness in them that our pain has pushed aside; and feel some compassion, not only for the hard journey they had but also for the pain we have caused them.

Commit to the journey

Getting to a forgiving place, finding the forgiving self inside us, is a long and complicated journey. We have to be ready to forgive. We have to want to forgive. The deeper the wound, the more difficult the process–which makes forgiving parents especially hard. Along the way, we may have to express our protest, we may have to be angry and resentful, and we may even have to punish our parents by holding a grudge. But when we get there, the forgiveness we achieve will be forgiveness worth having.

LETTING GO

There are occasions when we can only heal the hurt we feel our mother has inflicted on us by separating ourselves from her. But perhaps, if we can find a way to love our mothers just exactly as they are, generously and without expectation, we can make our way back to the embrace of that first beloved being: Mama.

You can't go to a dry well looking for water. It will be difficult to limit contact with your mother because like most daughters, many of us harbor a deep longing for her emotional approval. But at this point in your life, if she is not healthy enough to provide it; it's imperative that you let her go.

"Trust me, sometimes it's best to love your mother and then let her go," says fifty-one-year-old Jackie. "My mother was the most negative force in my life. And as soon as I removed her from my life, my whole world changed. It's hard to do, but sometimes you have to put your happiness and well-being before anyone else's. That's what I did and for the first time in my life, I am at peace."

My girlfriend, (who swore she'd disown me if I wrote her name), says her peace came from accepting the fact that her mother simply won't change.

"I don't even try to change her. But when you write *Help! I'm Recovering From My Mother*, let me know," she says.

REFLECTIONS

❧ Is there something about your mother that you need to forgive?
❧ If you have a great relationship with your mother, why do you think it has been so successful?

PART IV

Mother Stories

Almost everyone with a mother has a story to share. Be it good, bad, funny or embarrassing...our relationships with our mothers leave a lasting impression.

Here, some readers and writers share their stories, paying tribute, saying thanks, and exploring the good, the bad and ugly of their relationships with their mothers.

A mother like no other

By Sonya Patterson, for Wilma Patterson

I was four years old when Wilma Patterson rescued me—from my mother. I use the term "mother" sparingly because Norma Johnson was far from a mother, at least nowhere near what I believed a mother should be. Norma never wanted kids and she reminded me and my two siblings of that every day. We "cramped her style, cost too much money and were nothing but headaches."

Norma was quick to say such horrible things like, "I should've aborted ya'll asses."

I remember wanting to ask her, "Why did you have us, then?" But since Norma was prone to hurling whatever object was within her reach, I kept my little mouth closed. I kept it closed for years, but inside I was screaming, crying to be loved. I would've even settled for just feeling like someone cared about me. Don't get me wrong; my maternal grandmother tried. But she lived across the country and we seldom saw her because as Norma put it, that woman got on her "damn nerves." And don't even get me started on my daddy. Or my sister's daddy. Or my brother's daddy. Three different men and only my sister talked to her father. My brother and I didn't know who our fathers were. Norma didn't either. But even my sister's visits were few and far between because his "real" family didn't want to be reminded of a child created from an extramarital affair.

Wilma rescued me and my siblings from that horrible existence. Unable to have children of her own, she came across my brother digging through the trash in our apartment building, where she was visiting a friend. She took my brother back to our apartment and struck up a conversation with Norma. At first, Norma was standoffish, but Wilma never belittled her or talked down to her. And when Wilma offered her babysitting services, Norma was all too happy to oblige, even though Wilma was a complete stranger.

Wilma became a fixture in our lives and before we knew it, we were spending weeks at her home. One weekend when my mother didn't return to pick us up, I found myself silently wishing that she never returned at all. Wilma gave me love I so desperately needed. Three days after the time she was supposed to pick us up, Norma showed up looking haggard and high on drugs. I don't know what it was she said to Wilma; I just remember eavesdropping and hearing words like "fed up" and "borrow money." From the gist of it, it sounded like Norma was offering to sell us for a hundred dollars each. Wilma didn't give Norma any money, but she did go down to Social Services the next day. The next thing I knew, she sat us down and told us we'd be staying with her indefinitely while she tried to get legal guardianship. Norma never bothered to protest and eventually, Wilma adopted us. I was ecstatic. I was seven years old at the time. That very day she told us the adoption was final. I asked if I could call Wilma "Mama," since Norma would never allow it. With tears in her eyes, she replied, "Of course, baby."

That was thirty years ago.

I often wonder the path my life would have taken if God had not sent an angel named Wilma into our lives. All three of us went on to graduate from college. We all have successful, fulfilling careers. My sister does occasionally struggle with some issues of self-worth. I probably should, but Mama showed me so much love that Norma's lack of love is but a distant memory. I don't question why my birth mother was the way she was. I believe that it was all part of God's master plan. He knew Wilma needed us and we needed her.

So to my mother, Wilma, I thank you. For saving me. For loving me. For being a mother like no other.

Sonya Patterson is a teacher who resides in Washington, D.C.

A Stretch of Prayer

By Peggy Eldridge-Love, for Ruby Allen

I remember how excited we all were when, at seven, our entire neighborhood was preparing to move. My family and about six of our neighbors were relocating to a neighborhood about five miles away, while another nine or ten families were moving to other communities within close proximity of our new northeast location, too. We were all a part of a big movement that back then was called urban renewal. Our old homes were being taken and destroyed to make way for what was being touted as progress.

Years later, while sitting on the front porch of my family's new home, I was discussing with my mother a situation I was confronted with that did not seem to have a feasible solution. To my surprise, mother chuckled as I finished my hopeless, tearful lament. She said, "Baby, there isn't anything God can't do. There's nothing too hard for the Lord."

That wasn't the first time Mother had reminded me of God's omnipotence. It was a part of who and what she was to bear witness to Him, His love and His unchanging power. But there was something extra special in that chuckle that had preceded her comment, and I knew mother was about to share something very enlightening with me. I was right.

"Do you remember when you were seven and we moved from Perry Street here to Wyandotte Avenue?"

I assured her that I did. It was a memory etched in all of our minds, as it was such a landmark occasion. There was no comparison between the old neighborhood and the new. Making that move had been a quantum leap forward, not just for us, but also for all the families that had made it with us.

"Well, baby," she continued. "I desperately wanted to move our family away from Perry Street, but there was no way economically your father and I could afford to make any move at that time. There were things about living in that old neighborhood I know you don't remember. But as a mother, I knew they were things that could possibly limit and compromise my children's best interest. So I began to pray that the Lord would make a way for us to move."

It seemed in that moment I remembered a time or two of coming inside from playing and stumbling upon Mother on her knees in prayer, petitioning the Lord for just such a thing.

Mother chuckled again. "One day not long after I began to pray, a man came to our front door saying he had come to talk to your father and me about purchasing our property. He was from the government."

My mouth dropped. How well I remembered the tall man in the brown suit, carrying a briefcase walking down Perry Street that day so many years ago.

"You see, baby," Mother continued in her warm, soft voice, "God was sending through a whole turnpike in answer to my prayer. That man was from the highway department. They needed to buy our house, and all those around it so they could build the Kansas Turnpike. Yes, ma'am, God sent through a whole turnpike in answer to my prayer."

It has been decades since Mother shared that with me. But it was only a few days ago that I was in prayer about yet another circumstance that to my human mind and understanding didn't seem to have a solution. Suddenly, I heard myself utter, "Lord, I need a turnpike. Please, Lord, send me a turnpike."

As I realized what I said I felt the weight lift from my heart, and I began to chuckle. I felt certain that not only had the Lord heard my prayers, but He had already prepared the answer. He just wanted to make sure I remembered how big and awesome He is even when what we are asking for seems enormous. I have no doubt my own "turnpike" is on the way.

So, should ever find yourself traveling between Kansas City and Topeka on the I-70 Kansas Turnpike know that you are riding on a small stretch of prayer; it is God's answer to my mother's prayer.

Peggy Eldridge-Love is a poet, playwright, screenwriter and novelist. Her published works include You Beckon *and* The Knoll Frames.

Mirror Image?

BY K, FOR DOROTHEA J. WALKER

I'll bet you think you're gonna read a cheery story about how much alike a daughter and a mother have become, huh? Well, not this one.

My mother was a staunch Louisiana Republican, who took great pride in canceling my father's Democratic vote. I'm probably whatever the new third party is going to be, but in the meantime I'm an Independent and proud of it! Hmmm, is pride genetic?

Sure, Mom squeezed me out into loving arms and the light of the world and yes, she taught me to read, write, and tie my shoes, but that hardly qualifies us as being the Bobbsey Twins. We both like to eat and cook a good meal. Cheese and chocolate have a much deeper importance to the two of us than to most people, but other than those few things, Mom and I are species from opposite ends of the outer limits. It didn't start out that way though.

We started out closer than close, maybe even too close. Mom was where the laughs and lessons, kisses, and hugs were. She had the kind words and understanding. She was overflowing with life lessons and uncommon sense. Don't get me wrong, my daddy was a great father, but at four, she was my candy bowl. I could reach inside, whenever I needed a taste of sweetness and goodness from this world. What little girl in her right mind wouldn't want to *be* that?

Back during the tender years, she was all I ever wanted to be. Every single thing she did, I imitated to mirror perfection. I wanted to be exactly like her. It never occurred to me that there was anything else to be but a mommy and a wife...until Mark Twain Elementary School. As gut-wrenching as those first few days away from her were—a few graham crackers, a little milk, and a teacher who read stories aloud and sang after nap time, it soon smoothed my transition to my new world—a world where there were a bazillion other things to be, *besides* Mom. My mother even rewarded and encouraged my independence then, and reminded me over and over that she could have been more if she had studied just a little bit harder. She mentioned that she might have liked being a teacher.

So, of course, the first thing I wanted to be, other than her, was a teacher. Those dolls of mine started gettin' lessons right away. That tickled Mom to no end. She even played along cheerfully, until I decided to become Mr. Simpson, the booty-paddling principal. Okay, so I got a little bossy. It wasn't like she didn't have a belt hangin' out of her purse for those special occasions—when *the look* simply wasn't enough.

She stopped playing principal with me so I decided to be something else, altogether. I decided I wanted to be my best friend, Shelley. Shelley was the smartest girl in our whole school. Mom took my desertion well because she wanted me to be smart and have smart friends.

Unfortunately, smart children, like Shelley, often have smart mouths. I remember coming up from the sink full of dishwater, and a face full of suds after popping out one of Shelley's "way too grown" witticisms about the unfairness of chores. Mom was old school. She didn't play mouthy brat, so I picked someone else to be with quickness—her older sister, Karen.

Karen played the piano. I wanted to play the piano. Mom let me take piano lessons. Karen had a flip. I wanted a flip. Mom let me cut my hair into a flip when I went to the seventh grade. Karen wanted to be an obstetrician. I wanted to be an obstetrician. Mom never said I couldn't be a doctor, but she kept telling me that writing and drawing were my strengths. I pretended that I didn't hear and drowned her out of my mind. Karen was extremely popular and had a boyfriend. So when I asked if I could have a boyfriend, that's where my mother drew the line.

She said, "No boyfriends until you're sixteen, Daughter."

I'm sure she knew that I didn't really have anyone interested. I was just a gangly, goofy, nerdy seventh-grader, who thought that I was going to magically morph into Karen once puberty finished what it had started. When I never grew another millimeter after the sixth grade and got her breasts almost overnight that should have been a clue that Karen's lithe and limber body wasn't in my cards. Looking back, I know that I sensed its coming, and I fought it with everything in my arsenal, but every year that passed found me looking, talking, thinking, and acting more like my mother. So, I did what most teeny-boppers, struggling for individuality first, do: I set out to be her opposite.

During my mean teens, I tried to shed all evidence of our earlier closer than closeness to let her know that I intended to be myself. Never mind that I didn't have even a doodle about who I was or wanted to become. I just knew I didn't want to be them. Back in the day, I viewed my mother as well meaning but a corny throwback to old countrified ways and ancient rules that nobody used—at least not in junior high. Her nicey-nice Golden Rule crap got me in ankle-deep doodie. It didn't take long to realize that her sense of fairness was only good for two things in junior high school— irritating the hell out of the popular kids and getting teased, or an official beat down from the bigger and meaner ones. After a series of painfully long and miserable school days that found me taking alternate routes home, I decided to make a list of all the things I needed to change to make teen life bearable. I didn't understand it then, but I now know that I was trying to eliminate *her* from me:

Stop bringing my lunch—uncool

Stop listening to talk radio—very un-cool

Stop wearing Mommy-made clothes—uncool

Start wearing popular clothes and hairdos

Get a job

No more oatmeal for breakfast. Oatmeal is for babies.

We went ten brutal rounds about the lunch bag thing. Mom demanded reasons. I didn't really have any good ones, other than "nobody cool carries their lunch," but I knew that kind of excuse would fly as high as pot-bellied pig with her. The last thing on earth that Dorothea J. Walker cared about was what 'cool people' did. So when she backed me into the corner with her usual machine-gun blast of questions, I actually fixed my little premenstrual mouth to say, "Only poor people bring their lunches to school, Mom!" Somehow she managed to hear me out without giving me *"the look,"* which was actually progress because by junior high, we could give each other a look that sent each other into a blazin' rage. Unfortunately for me, only one of us got a chance to express that kind of emotion and keep their mouth attached to her face.

Anyway, she chuckled a little after my poignant observation and replied, "But, baby…we are poor." That was it. She ended our discussion just like that. I went to my room and cried until I couldn't cry another tear. Somehow, she must have heard and felt my pain because the next morning—no lunch bag.

Where my despised hand-cut bologna and cheese sandwich once sat on the pale-green tiled counter, in its 'recycled before recycling was popular' brown bag, stood a short stack of quarters—shining like the silver sun of a brand-new day. Yeah, Baby! Daughter 1 / Mom 0.

Our Christmas wish-list chat solved my "talk radio" dilemma. I never completely understood why, but Mom loved listening to the news. News, news, news, and mo' badder news. Every now and then she'd turn on some music but it wasn't even close to "cool" music that "cool" people listened to. It was that old corny jazz and blues that she and Dad liked—that dated crap that made Aunt Ollie jump up and do that goofy hootchie coochie dance with Uncle Diamond, after two cups of "adult only" homemade eggnog; Z.Z. Hill, Bobby Blue Bland, Koko Taylor, and Etta James. You know what I'm talkin' about—"parent music." I wanted to hear *my* generation's music: The Temps, The Four Tops, Martha and The Vandellas, and Stevie Wonder. She hadn't even finished asking what I wanted for Christmas, before I blurted, "A transistor radio!" They were expensive back then (seven whole dollars), but I assured her that I didn't want anything else, so she agreed. Whoo! Hoo! Daughter 2 / Mom 0.

Mom was very proud of the fact that she sewed every last stitch of her family's clothing, down to our drawers, so I broke my desire for store-bought clothes to her gently. After months of hinting, I massaged my way into asking if I could get a job so I could buy my own clothes. There! I'd said it! I felt like a pile of fresh crap when I saw the deep hurt and pink glaze in her hazel eyes. But she shook it off like Muhammad Ali and said she would talk to my father about it.

I was actually gullible enough to think I had won and was runnin' things in my life. Even though I didn't feel good about hurting my mother's feelings, by being an ungrateful brat, I knew I'd feel better when I had on a nice white pair of Go-Go boots and a jersey knit jumper, like the Beatle-banged girls in *Seventeen* magazine. Back then, even in the ghetto, the Beatles had a little "juice."

About three weeks later, Mom pulled me aside and said, "Your father and I decided you could get a job as long as you keep your grades up. Oh, and you can start buying your own clothes, but your father and I must approve of them."

My grades had always been A's with a spattering of B's. That would be a piece of pineapple upside-down cake. I knew enough of what was acceptable to squeak by their dress code and patted myself on the back for having catapulted myself into adulthood ahead of schedule. No more asking anybody for anything! No more "Yes, Ma'am" and "No, Sir!" I had my own clothes, my own shoes, and my own money! I was the "Big Baller-Shot Caller!" Right? Wrong!

I loved going to work. I felt so mature. I loved stacking up those dirty little green pieces of paper into my "cool" purse that I bought with my own money. Just when I was mid-flight on the road to freedom and popularity, I got a "C" in math and she gave my lil' leash a yank that almost decapitated me. My loving my job was just the leverage Mom needed to whip me right back into shape. If I wavered, she warned once. Mom 1 / Daughter 2. And those store-bought clothes? She won that one, too.

Why were my clothes falling apart in the wash? Why didn't they fit? Why did it cost so much money to put them in the cleaners? Why was my baby sister borrowing them before I even got a chance to take the price tag off? Why couldn't I find anything to wear to the ninth-grade graduation dance? She calmly listened to my long list of woes and agreed to make me a light-blue mohair, three-piece suit out of this bolt of material that Dad won in a card game.

It was definitely the coolest thing she'd ever made me. It was the season's most popular color—baby blue. It was the season's most popular fabric—mohair. It was the season's most popular cut—double-breasted vest and straight skirt—and just for giggles, she made me a fully lined, knee-length matching walking coat to go with it. I was the living, breathing talk of the dance. The oldest and coolest of cool girls crowded around me and asked where I got my walking suit. I told them my mother made it, and they immediately asked if she sewed for other people. When I was priming her up to make me a few more items, I told her all the nice things the cool girls had said about my suit. Little did I know the reason she had gone so far out of her way was because it was the very last stitch she'd ever sew for me. She said, "You're getting harder and harder to please. I'll teach you to sew for yourself, though."

I tried to suppress my sheer and utter fear at the notion of having to learn how to sew for myself, just to have clothes that didn't eat up my whole little paycheck or fall apart at the seams. Surely, she had seen my unfinished gym bag *and* apron. Was this some cruel joke? I was to needle and thread what chimpanzee is to a chess set.

Somehow, at the time when we were growing further and further apart, she trained me step by step to sew well enough to save a little money and still keep decent clothes on my back. Mom 2/ Daughter 2. That left oatmeal.

From September to damn near May, Monday through Friday, every morning the sun shined, it rained, or anything in between, Mom had a quart-sized pot of oatmeal rattling its lid on the stove.

When we asked for extra brown sugar, she'd say, "You don't need to add anything. I've already added enough sugar, butter, and milk." Pre-adding the extras cut two apples with one knife; it saved on expensive items and it cut out waste and excessive use of things she didn't think were healthy for us. Don't you worry your meaty little heads about taste and texture.

My first inclination was to take the noble path and just tell her, "Mom, you cook a mean pot of gumbo, a super serious pan of cinnamon rolls from scratch, and a Saturday casserole that's to die for, but your oatmeal?" I didn't want to hurt her feelings again, so I took an easy out and started buying a nice big box of Captain Crunch, and with my own money.

When I first brought it in the house and sat it on top of the refrigerator, I'll be honest, it felt good. I felt like I was finally in charge of my own life and destiny. I felt like I had taken the oatmeal dealio by the horns and solved one of my biggest problems in life. As I gobbled bowl after sugary bowl, I swelled with pride like a water balloon on the Fourth of July. Only sixteen, and I was handling things like an adult, or so I thought.

I should have known something was up when Mom watched me devouring mountains of Captain Crunch and Cocoa Pebbles without saying a word, but looking like—you know that smug little look mothers get when you're wrong and they're right, but they don't really come out and say it—like that! Something was up, but what?

The first thing that was up was my cereal-swiping siblings. I'd buy a king-sized box on Sunday and by Wednesday that baby was totaled-out. Everyone swore, "It wasn't me!" One day, when I doubled back to get an assignment I left on the dining room table, I caught my father chowing down a great big mixing bowl of my cereal. How could I tell my father not to eat *my* cereal when he had paid for everything that ever went inside my body since birth? I did mention it to Mom, but she just laughed and said, "He's so vain. He's picking up weight, *too*. When his belt gets a little tighter, he'll leave it alone, baby."

"Gaining weight...too?" There are no years more vain than sixteen, except seventeen, eighteen, and nineteen. You best believe I headed straight for the mirror. It didn't take long to see why my waistbands had started to cinch and pinch, and all my zippers were starting to pop. She was right! I had porked up nicely, with my Captain Crunch-eatin' self.

I had never had a weight problem before, but I remember Mom talking about losing weight. I went straight to the source. Naturally, she tried to put me back on that slimy oatmeal, but I just couldn't stomach another bowl. I went on boiled eggs and tomato slices and toast for about a month and, being young, I bounced right back into shape. Mom 3/ Daughter 2.

I lost my mother three years after that to breast cancer. There really aren't words to express how much her love and Mommy tricks were missed. My father, two brothers, younger sister, then fifteen, and I staggered through life with a piece, the size of a small solar system, ripped out of our lives. For the longest time, I thought I was pedaling on my own, but she was right behind me—still running and holding up the bike with all the things she taught me, and all the things she said...and didn't say. She was really some-one special. Maybe I'm not her identical twin, but we do have a lot more in common. Sometimes I brown bag it; I hate the news but love talk radio; and I buy my clothes. I have a few made for special occasions. Mom would laugh to tears knowing that even though I only eat oatmeal once or twice a week, for all the gold in Ghana, I couldn't eat a bowl of Captain Crunch. Mom 4/ Daughter 2. What? I still work every day! Do the math! ~wink!~

K is the alter ego of author Kweli Walker. A resident of Los Angeles, her next book, an Afroerotic novel called At The End of Silence *will be released in March 2006.*

When the Time is Right
BY J. MYSTERY, FOR DOROTHY

"Ma, when are we leaving?"

"Soon, baby, soon."

"Okay, Ma, I'll go pack."

Into a cluttered room I'd rush my size 11's to gather the things a ten-year-old loves most. With hopes of never returning to this awful place I called home, I'd gather my prettiest dress, some barrettes for my out-of-control hair, underwear (the training bras especially), a fully equipped book bag, and my toothbrush. It was enough for my skinny frame to manage in such short notice. I had to move fast; we were getting out of this place, and there was no time to waste.

"I'm ready, Ma. We can go now?"

Her eyes were sad but her smile was always bright. I knew she loved him. I knew she'd known him almost all her life. But I also knew he made her cry late into the night. I knew he shrunk her—my beloved mother—and all I wanted as I stood there in the small kitchen of our modest home in the Northeast section of the Bronx, anxious to escape the daily drama that festered in my tiny world— the constant fighting, the continuous arguing and verbal abuse, the struggling, the violent mood swings, the confusion— all I wanted was to stop the pain and the fear that became a constant in our lives. All I wanted was for Mommy and me to laugh again, be happy and independent again. All I wanted was my mother back—the strong, confident beauty who never had to yell to tell you off; the petite woman who appeared giant-like in her stance in this life. But the man who was not my father— somehow, some way—stole that from me.

Somehow, some way, he shrunk the unshrinkable woman.

"Soon, baby," she said again, pulling me into her warmth, forcing out a soft chuckle.

"When, Ma? When? What time? Don't you wanna leave, too?" I asked, trying to make sense of her hesitation.

"Yes, baby."

"So we're really leaving, right? You promise?" I tried to fight the tears as disappointment made its grand entrance.

"I promise, baby. When the time is right."

"When will that be, Ma?"

"Soon, baby, soon."

For almost ten years, Mom and I would have this same dialogue and for almost ten years I'd find myself packing and unpacking, praying that "soon" would come one day, and she'd finally get the courage to leave him and his part-time kids. He wasn't rich. He was okay-looking but not Denzel by a longshot, and he carried heavy luggage and major drama. *What could she possibly see in him?* I thought over and over to myself as I tried desperately not to resent her. I began to wonder if she loved me at all. Her staying seemed like a selfish act to my young mind.

Finally, it was time for me to head off to college. I promised myself that this would be the last time I packed my bags and finally, with or without my mother, I was leaving.

It was a bright sunshiny day in June as I began packing to begin my summer studies away. I stayed in my room for what seemed like hours making sure I had everything I needed. The house was quieter than usual. I knew my stepfather and his kids weren't there, but I wondered where my mother could be.

After a while I walked out of my room and was about to go down the narrow hallway and down the stairs to the basement to see if my mother was there sewing as usual, but I never made it that far. I was stunned by what I saw as I stood frozen in the hallway. It was my mother standing with her back to the door of her adjacent bedroom—packing, too. With clothes sprawled out over the bed, she looked at my teary eyes and smiled.

And just like that I got it. I understood the tears, the pain, the fake laughter to soften the tough journey, the sacrifices. She wasn't being selfish or weak; what she was doing was just what she had promised she'd do. Leave when the time was right. I instantly understood what patience is and what patience does and more importantly, I understood my mother's love.

Today, as I go through life being the stepmother I never wanted to be, I often chuckle softly at how my mother's strength has become my strength. I never thought I'd see the day I'd be making the same sacrifices and choices she did—loving a man and his child and at times putting my own needs to the side. Although my relationship is not abusive, I have her lessons of choice and chance.

I did not choose my destiny, but chance has it that I am strong enough to handle it. My mother could have chosen to leave each time I pleaded, but how many times would we have had to return? I could have said "no" when my husband asked me to marry him, but I decided being like my mother wasn't such a bad thing. She made sure my future was secure and now it's the future that motivates me. As I consider my options as a mother, I don't feel so bad when, like my mother, I have to sit back and wait for the right time to do certain things. Like her, I, too, can now see the bigger picture of life. I chose to make the house a home first—the love, I chose to first receive before I could give; the security, I had to believe was possible.

Now, when I finally do have a child, they will see the sacrifices and even if they, too, are anxious to move on, I will know from the lessons I learned from my mother that I did what I could to make sure they were ready for whatever the future holds.

"Ma, are we leaving now?"

"Yes it's time, baby, let's go."

J. Mystery is a proposal writer and ghostwriter currently at work on her first novel.

Deciding to Dance

BY TRINA MCREYNOLDS, FOR SOFIA MCREYNOLDS

I nterracial dating was still quite taboo in the late 1960s as our country struggled with the issue of race. For this reason, it was quite unexpected when my father, an African-American soldier training for his tour of duty during the Vietnam War; and my mother, a recent high school graduate, met and fell in love during this tumultuous time. When their love led to pregnancy, it was with great courage that my mother married a man whom she expected that her Mexican-American family would reject. With time and love, two families and two cultures eventually became one.

Admittedly, as the product of an interracial marriage, the awkward years of adolescence were even more acutely painful for me. I struggled mightily to be accepted by my peers when our family wasn't like any other family in our community. I remember vividly the consoling words of my mother when in the sixth grade, my date to the school dance called to tell me that he couldn't go because his parents didn't approve of their son escorting a black girl. My mom did more than share my tears and attempt to assuage my pain. She used that experience as an opportunity to teach me a life lesson that I still hold dear to this day.

She told me that I had a choice to make: 1) I could go to the dance, try my best to enjoy myself with my friends, and believe that there would be other dances and other dates; or 2) I could feel sorry for myself and not go to the dance now that I was dateless and disappointed. My mother told me that if I chose option one, I was choosing life, which meant embracing the good and learning from the bad. She told me that if I chose option two, I was choosing to accept "life's leftovers." Mom explained that "life's leftovers" were simply the unused remnants of experiences not worthy of those who chose life. Since that day, I have embraced my mother's words and have always chosen life.

To my mom, Sofia McReynolds, for being ingenious in always making a way to buy new clothes for school when there wasn't money for that luxury; for being resourceful in learning to apply relaxers and use flat irons to help tame my unruly mane; and for always being inventive in your advice and counsel. I live my life as a tribute to you.

Trina McReynolds is an attorney and aspiring writer residing in Plano, Texas.

Thanks to my Mom

By Vanessa Johnson, for
Arcadia "Grace" Woods Alexander
January 12, 1932 – August 28, 1994

L ess than six months into my marriage, I packed my belongings and went back to my parents' home after a huge argument with my husband. My mother never asked me any questions as to why I left or what happened.

That same night she sat me down and said, "Look, don't listen to what anybody says. Only you know what you have at home, so base your decision to return on that and not what anybody else says."

To this day, that was the best piece of advice I could have received. My husband and I have been married for over twenty-six years, and we are still together thanks to that piece of advice. Not only did my mother's words help me to make a decision that night to return to my husband, but I've based other decisions in my life on it as well. Only I know what I have at home. I won't let anybody tell me a thing about what goes on inside my house. Thanks, Mom! I miss you like crazy.

Vanessa Johnson is the self-published author of When Death Comes Knocking. *She lives in Louisiana.*

Grandma's Diva

BY ANGIE PICKETT HENDERSON, FOR SUE DEVEREAUX

When I sat down to write my story, I knew whatever I wrote would have to be something that captured the very essence of the sole person responsible for the diva that I've grown into today. Whatever was written would have to be just as truthful and candid as the woman that I am so proud to have turned into—my mother's mother.

When you are close to another person you just know when something "ain't right." First of all, I talk to my grannie at least every other day. So after three days had passed and I wasn't able to get in touch with her, I knew something was wrong. Finally, on day four, I received a call from my grandmother stating that she'd passed out and had been in Princeton Hospital for the past few days. Immediately my husband and I rushed to New Jersey.

Upon walking into my grandmother's hospital room, I was greeted by the sounds of her husky voice, "I don't like the way you are talking to me. Go and get your damned supervisor."

Gerard, my husband, stifled a laugh. I turned to him to see what was so funny and he mouthed the words, "She's just like you!" I rolled my eyes at him since I didn't find anything he was saying remotely funny. I was horrified by what I was hearing and quickly went to speak to the nurse with whom my grandmother was having the confrontation. After dealing with the situation, I walked over to my grandmother's bed and looked down to kiss her. While staring down into her face, it hit me so hard I almost fell over. "Oh my God, this is me, fifty years from now."

My husband's comment made me mad because it was true. And the truth hurts.

Like so many African-American children born out of wedlock, my grand-mother raised me. My mother conceived me during her sophomore year of college at the age of nineteen. Clearly too young and naïve to be anyone's mother, my grandmother quickly volunteered to take her grandbaby and raise her. I was the type of little girl that she'd always wanted. My mother was such a shy and introverted child that my grandmother always felt that her ways were more like my grandfather's. But even at the tender age of six days, my grandmother knew that I was the little prissy, smart-mouthed, spoiled baby that she'd always wanted. It was just her and me for so many years, and she was the most influential person during the formative years of my life. I can honestly say that no matter how many vocal coaches, teachers, French tutors, boyfriends or professors that I've encountered, no one affected the world the way my grandma did.

Any time I reflect on my grandmother, four major things come to mind:

Her sharp tongue. The general rule in my family was that once my grand-mother got through cussing you out, you'd never be the same.

The fact that she was a clothes horse. My grandmother had a room in her house that had nothing but racks of clothes and shoes.

Her great love affair with the arts.

How she could cook a meal to make you fall in love with her on the spot.

All of these things are a major part of my life now.

My mouth has been described as sassy, bold, brazen, fresh, filthy, and a whole lot of other things. But the bottom line is that most of the things that fall from lips tend to be some variation of a comment that I once heard my grandmother use. Sometimes I will use a saying and people will look at me in awe like, "Child, that's some old folks' stuff right there." And I will just smile because I know that it is. I call those comments my "Grandma Suisms" because they are sayings that came straight from her.

My love of clothing has probably been one of my biggest downfalls in life. I remember when I got my very first charge card. I went out and charged it up to the limit in two days on clothes. My justification was that I NEEDED everything that was in those shopping bags. Oh, my grandmother was steaming like grits. She cussed me up and down the street, but after all was said and done, she sat on her bed and laughed until I thought she was crazy. "Child, I can't be mad at you 'cause you come by it honestly. Lord knows we can't pass up nothing pretty," she said.

Grandma's fondness for the arts and things that she likes to call "cultured" manifested itself in me. Since she grew up in the South, got married young and had two children back to back, she was never really able to study music like she wanted to, so by age four I was taking voice lessons and singing solos in church. By the time I was seven, I was taking piano, voice, cello and violin lessons. Broadway plays were another big thing with her. I remember whining and crying about wanting to go see a movie, and she would tell me "common folk do the movies. Cultured folk do the theater." I remember one time I was so tired of hearing that mess, I asked her when I would be able to be common because it seemed as if they had more fun. Needless to say that warranted one of those famous Grandma Sue slaps.

Truly though, the one thing that most people in my family think about when they have thoughts of my grandmother are her culinary skills. She would always cook big meals from scratch. I never ever remember eating stuff out of cans or packages. My grandmother used to always say that meals made from scratch were meals made with love. I have never forgotten that saying, and I have committed it to heart and memory. Every meal that I make I can honestly say started from scratch, and I have that sassy-mouthed, sharp-dressing, music-loving North Carolina sister to thank for that. Needless to say that's the one trait that my husband thoroughly enjoys my inheriting from her.

Angie Pickett Henderson is the president of Adeeva Publicity. Visit her website at www.adeevapub.com.

"Mama, I'm Sorry"

BY NADIA MONROE, FOR LAURA JOHNSON

They are two little words—words that can't even begin to sum up all that I've done wrong. *I'm sorry*. For the pain I caused you—I'm sorry. For the tears you shed— I'm sorry.

My mother is one of those who did everything right. Yet, I still did everything wrong. My father died when I was a baby and my mother struggled to raise my brother and me. She kept a tight reign on me, but not too tight where I rebelled. She was in my life constantly asking me questions, trying to meet my friends. She tried to talk to me and worked overtime to get me to walk the straight and narrow. She didn't work too much on her job or give too little of her time. She didn't neglect me, nor was there a lack of love. She set examples. She did everything right.

And still I did wrong.

I started at the age of fourteen, when I used to sneak out of the house after my mother went to sleep. I'd go hang out with my friends—friends who were headed no place fast. And trouble followed us like a hungry tomcat. Where trouble didn't follow us, we made it. My mother was at her wit's end. She tried punishing me, lecturing me, even whipping me. Nothing worked.

At fourteen, I took my first trip to jail. Shoplifting some clothes I really didn't need. Actually, it was a juvenile facility, but judging from the look of sheer horror on my mother's face, it might as well have been Alcatraz. I would make two more trips before my seventeenth birthday. My mother even tried the tough love approach, making me stay for a few days. But still nothing worked.

My mother used to always sob, "Where did I go wrong?" I could never answer her then. But I can now. You didn't go wrong. You did everything a parent is supposed to do. You loved me, nurtured me, disciplined me. Every once in a while there comes a child, that despite all of that, still travels the wrong path. I was that child.

But through it all, my mother never gave up in terms of her love for me. That was a constant. Don't get me wrong; she didn't enable me. In fact, on my last trip to juvey, she told me how much she loved me, but I would have to learn on my own, because she was through.

I have finally learned. Too bad it took seven years in prison for me to do so. Too bad I hurt so many people along the way. I don't know why I traveled down the wrong path, hung out with the wrong people, loved the wrong man and ultimately ended up doing time. All I know is I finally want to live my life right. I *will* live my life right. I just wish my mother were here to see it.

To my mother—I will live my life as a tribute to you. Finally.

Nadia Monroe is an aspiring writer who lives in Atlanta, Ga.

Laughter is always best

BY J. MANGUM, FOR RUTH MANGUM

My Mom and I were at the doctor's office one day. I was about eleven, and I went in for a checkup. I had to sit and wait before giving a urine sample. The office was over by Duke University, so a lot of students and in-training doctors were around. My Mom is normally the type of woman who always keeps her composure; she is very lady-like.

Well, the student nurse came out and told me they were going to check my vagina. Mind you, my mom is old school, so words like vagina were not spoken around our house; it was called your "self" or your "privates." I sat still for a moment puzzled, and then I leaned over and whispered to my mom, "What is a vagina?" My mom looked at me and began to smile and said, "They are talking about your female area."

I thought for a moment, and then I looked back at her again and said, "Oh, I thought they were talking about my bottom." Tears began to flow from her eyes, and as she began to cry, so did I. Within the next few minutes, my Mom and I had the entire waiting room laughing in tears, and they had no idea what we were laughing about. I love my mom for that moment, and I am in tears right now, just thinking about it.

I guess this is a life lesson from my mom as well; truly laughter is the best medicine!

J. Mangum is the self-published author of On the Other Side of Through *and a contributor to the compilation book,* The Lost Sheep. *She resides in North Carolina.*

Cerebral Chaos

BY JAMES W. LEWIS, FOR PHYLLIS LEWIS

"No!" my mother yelled, her finger inches from my face. "You can't go outside! You're on restriction for a week!"

Rage warped my young face. Steam probably wafted out my ears because I swear my blood boiled upon hearing the horrid word "restriction." It should be illegal to ban a vivacious eleven-year-old boy from his BMX bike and his buddies—especially at the start of a new summer season!

But that's what I got for disobeying my mother. She told me to be home at two in the afternoon. I didn't come home until seven that evening.

With my eyes blurred from tears, I stomped out the living room toward my bedroom. I barely got to the doorway before a hard grip around my elbow curtailed forward progress.

"Don't you walk away from me!" My mother pointed toward the leather couch. "Sit down!"

I folded my wire-thin arms across my chest, my forehead furrowed. I turned to the couch and slammed my bottom on the cushion.

"Oh, okay," my mother said, nodding. "Since you think you can ruin the couch I paid for, you can't sit there. Get up!"

Oh, so now we were playing musical chairs. I rolled my eyes and stood up.

She grabbed my wrist. We walked through the kitchen into the small dining room area. "Sit in that chair."

I pulled out a chair from the dining table, plopped down, and fixated on the wall in front of me. I hated pushing my spine against the chair's curved iron backside, but I ignored the slight discomfort and leaned back. And my defiance wouldn't have been complete without my folded arms and pouty lips.

My mother walked over to a kitchen drawer and pulled out a pen and pad of paper. "I have an assignment for you."

My eyebrows shot up. *Assignment?* I thought. *School is over!*

She dropped the pad and pen in front of me. The wrinkles in my forehead grew deeper.

"You must be a genius," my mother said, grinning. "Something in that brilliant, hard-headed noggin of yours convinced you it was a good idea to come home so late."

I gazed at her, head tilted, trying to figure out what she had up her sleeve.

"So," she continued, "since you obviously have a creative mind, I want to see it on paper. I want you to write a story every night of your punishment… starting tonight."

I twisted my face and stared at the paper, then looked up at her.

"What do you want me to write about?" I asked.

"Anything you want. You have an hour, and I'll read it when you're done." She turned her back to me and walked into the kitchen. "I'll warm up your dinner, so get ta steppin'."

Talk about ball and chain. It was bad enough that I had to stay in the house; now my mother wanted to torture me. No TV, no ATARI, no handheld video games. Just me, the dining room table, a pen and a blank pad of paper.

I grabbed the pen. With a scowl, I transferred my anger through my thin fingers—and wrote. I didn't really care about plot or structure; I only wanted my revenge on paper.

My hand didn't stop. I wrote myself in as the main character and hero; my mother became the wretched villain and enemy to kids of the world. And, dang it, she was a villain! What cruel woman would keep her child inside the house with a world of adventure outside?

Of course, I defeated the "evil" villain with supersonic weapons.

I ate as I wrote and I finished an hour later. My mother sat down and read my story. She asked why I showed bad things happening to her. I didn't respond, just shrugged. My eyes fixated on the wall again, bottom lip sticking out. With a face still rife with fury, talking to her was the last thing on my mind.

To my surprise, my mother said she loved the story and couldn't wait to read another one tomorrow night. I sucked in my bottom lip to keep from smiling. Dang it, I was still mad at her! I couldn't let her see me smile!

But I felt good inside. I'd written a story, something I'd never done before—and my mother praised my effort.

The next night, I banged out another story. Mom was still a villain, but this time I used my super powers to manipulate her mind and made her my ally.

Mom read my story. As her eyes scanned the page, the corners of her lips raised and never fell. She even chuckled once or twice. Again, she praised my art of storytelling. She kissed my forehead, and I felt my hard resolve against her slipping away.

The third night, I started writing a little earlier than usual. An idea had been bouncing around in my head all day, and my body itched to create another "masterpiece."

My fingers whipped across the page and within minutes, I had created a story about preventing a kid from taking his own life. I'd seen a TV special on teenage suicide once, and I always wished I had the power to prevent such tragedy.

A look of sadness draped my mother's face. After she finished reading my story, she wrapped her arms around me and told me she loved me. I didn't ask how she felt about the story. I could see it in her glassy eyes.

Sleep didn't come easy that night. So many characters crystallized and swam in my head, much like in my dreams. I could see their faces; hear their voices; knew their likes and dislikes—everything.

And they wanted out.

Luckily, I had brought the pen and paper with me. With so much tug-of-war in my mind, I had plenty of ideas to create another story for my mother to read the following night. I wrote a story for myself this time.

The next few days, the stories kept coming. I looked forward to my mother's comments, but I didn't have to wait on the hour my mother had allotted for writing. I had plenty of time to write in my room. And with so much "cerebral chaos," I could create any adventure I wanted. Being stuck in the house couldn't limit my mind.

That same cerebral chaos stayed with me even after my mother lifted the outdoors ban. It carried on through my teenage years—and lives with me today as a man. The characters in my head still hold me captive some-times—until I release them. Only this time, I use a keyboard instead of pen and pad to set them free.

My mother knew what she was doing. She used the slick skills of Mr. Miyagi from the movie *The Karate Kid,* when Mr. Miyagi taught Daniel-Son karate lessons while Daniel-Son completed household chores. My mother helped unleash an untapped talent that filtered my wild imagina-tion through my fingers. During those seven days, I didn't see myself on restriction anymore.

I never told my mother the reason why I was so late that day twenty years ago. In the downtown library, it was easy to lose track of time in the won-drous world of Encyclopedia Brown, Charlie Brown and Snoopy, and choose-your-own-fate adventure books.

I still immerse myself in books, and sometimes, my mother buys me books for my birthday or for Christmas. But I also create my own novel-length manuscripts, now. And although I haven't published a novel yet, the thrill of seeing my name in print doesn't drive me. Cerebral chaos does—thanks to my mother's "assignments."

James W. Lewis is an up-and-coming author living in California. Visit his website at www.jameswlewis.com.

My Mother, Myself

BY DERA WILLIAMS, FOR VIVIAN ANN ROWLAND JONES

"Ladies don't chew gum in public."

"Ladies sit with their legs closed."

"Girls don't call boys."

How many times did I hear these phrases, or rather mandates from my mother while growing up? In Mom's way of thinking, there was a certain decorum of behavior that young women were supposed to adhere to. Raised in the Southern tradition of the 1930s and 40s, the oldest of two girls and seven boys in Arkansas, Mom was following the "rules" her mother had taught her. Properly raised Southern woman that she is, Mom was bound and determined to pass the rules on to her daughters. Since I was the oldest, I got the brunt of it. Southern women, black and white, can be steel magnolias but are known to be delicate and traditional and expected to be ladylike, she taught.

I remember one day we watched a woman sitting at a bus stop, puffing away on a cigarette.

"I hate to see a woman smoking on the streets. Ladies do not smoke in public," my mother said with a scowl.

My mother was also adamant that girls should not call boys. She came by her "rules" not only from her mother, but from her college days at a traditionally black college where convention was expected. There was a curfew; a dress code (they had to wear hose, no socks on campus); and mandatory vespers (church service). There were certain hours when company was taken, and there was a rule about how one dressed when going to town.

One of the Southern sayings my mother used when the conversation veered into my dating or courting was "Who are his people?" We were now in California but never mind; I was expected to tell her who the young man's family was and what his daddy did for a living. At times I thought my mother's mandates were hard and unyielding. When other girls were outside skating or riding bikes on a Saturday morning, I was either getting ready to go to the theater or to a ballet or piano lesson; playing came later. "You need to be exposed to culture," she would say.

I find that as my daughter, who is now in her mid-twenties, approached adolescence the world had changed since we baby boomers came of age. Generation X women think nothing of asking a young man out, picking him up, and in some cases ready to fight another woman in public about a man. Hmmm. What is wrong with this picture? Suddenly strange maxims were coming out of my mouth. "Who are his people that didn't teach him how to properly court a woman?" and "Nice boys don't respect girls who don't conduct themselves like ladies in public." Ooops, did I say that? Were those words coming from my mouth? Was my body fusing into my mother's? I have been told the older I get, the more I look like her. How much more I'm like her.

Despite my daughter's assertion in her teens and early twenties that my views were old-fashioned, antiquated and not politically correct, I was unwavering. My daughter complained that my beliefs did not fit in with the new dating scene. Yet, it made me proud when she came to me and said, "Mom, you are right. When I go out and see how these women my age act out in public, I am thankful that you told me the things you did and exposed me to how a woman is supposed to conduct herself."

One day I heard her tell a friend in a telephone conversation, "Maybe I'm old-fashioned but a man has to court me; none of that me picking up the tab or Dutch treat unless we are in a committed relationship."

So what came out of all those prissy "rules" my mother taught me? A realization that all and all, Mom did have some valid points. Just maybe the old-school standards are worthy of taking note as I see it come full circle. I like tea parties and write thank-you notes in longhand; so does my daughter.

And I do not wear white shoes after Labor Day. And guess what, neither does my daughter.

California native Dera Williams is a writer who has had stories published in A Cup of Comfort for Women *and* Life Spices for Seasoned Sistahs.

Life lessons Mama taught me
By Pat Tucker, for Deborah Tucker

Most daughters can thank their mothers for important life lessons such as how to cook and clean; the importance of manners; how to respect themselves and others; as well as an understanding and appreciation for a higher power. While I too can and do thank my mother, Deborah Tucker, for all of the above and more, there's one more important thing I will forever be grateful to her for. Growing up here in the U.S. like most young people, I had no true understanding of the freedom and opportunities I took for granted. This did not become apparent until a recent visit to my mother's homeland. When I visited Belize, Central America—not the tourist sections lined with fancy resorts and hotels, but the parts where people living in shacks struggle hard for the little they have every day—I learned there is no way I'd ever be able to thank my mother enough for the sacrifices she made to ensure my freedom. I had opportunities that were not afforded to her in the Third World country she called home. In that country education does not come free. There is no government assistance of any kind; and young girls and women do not drive. With a low-educated population, teen pregnancy is the norm, and women believe it is okay to have as many children as their bodies can produce. While my mother was born in that country with fifteen brothers and sisters, she knew she wanted a better life for herself but mainly for her children. So now when I visit my mother's homeland, as a college-educated TV journalist dreaming of publishing success and much more, I have my mother to thank for her determination and persistence. She worked hard to make sure her daughters would be able to take full advantage of every freedom and opportunity generations of women in her country will never know, much less experience firsthand. I'll begin to thank my mother by passing the legacy she began onto my own daughter.

Pat Tucker is a journalist and author of When Loved Ones Lie. *She lives in Houston, TX. Visit her website at www.rekcutppublishing.com.*

One of a Kind

BY DEIADRA JONES, FOR DELLA N. JONES BILLINGSLEY

"Don't answer the door."

"Don't look out the windows."

"When I call the phone will ring twice; I'll hang up, then call back."

"Dinner is already prepared, eat at seven, and give your brothers and sisters baths at seven-thirty and have everybody in bed by eight. Is that understood?"

To this day, those sentences continue to dance in my head. They were the familiar words my mother constantly said to me starting from the time I was six years old. At that time my mother, a recent divorcee, was a part-time student at the local community college, part-time RN at the nursing home, and a full-time mother to five children.

That's enough to break even the strongest of women. But my mother "held it down." She did her best to make sure her children had the same things that other children had. Even though we were poor, we never went without a meal, clothes on our back, or a roof over our heads. I know sometimes she may think we're ungrateful, but we wouldn't trade her for anything in the world. She instilled moral and family values in us that have shaped us all into the individuals we are today.

My mother made a very important and productive impact on my life, not just because she's my mother, but because she's a strong woman who never depended on anyone other than herself to raise her children. As a family we used to sit down and talk on Friday evenings about things that went on during the week and about things in general such as friends, school, and plans for the weekend. They are times I will always treasure. Now don't get me wrong; growing up in my house wasn't peaches and cream. Mama was a firm believer in not sparing the rod to spoil the child and was quick to pull out a stick and use it if she had to.

She wasn't an abusive mother; she just demanded respect and believe me when I say she got it! She ran a very strict house and no one dared to question her authority. Some of her rules were hard to deal with as a teenager.

For example: it was graduation night and surprisingly, she let me out of the house but I had to be in by midnight. Well, as you probably know the party had just started when it was time for me to go home. So I took it upon myself to stay out a little longer. Bad move! When I did get in around three, my mother was waiting for me in the living room on the couch with the lights off and with a teapot in her hand. (I guess that was the first thing she grabbed) and as soon as I opened the door she… Well, for the sake of Child Protective Services, I'll leave the rest to your imagination. Let's just say to this day I only drink instant tea.

Mama's rules and regulations taught me patience and endurance because they didn't bend, break, or bruise for anybody. Nevertheless, she's a great mother and is greatly appreciated for the things she has contributed to my life. I have the utmost respect for my mother because she always takes care of her business.

She's had a hard life so that my siblings and I could have a happy and productive childhood, and I thank her for that. She's taught us to never settle for less than what we're worth. She also taught us to take time and think about everything we do because any choice that has to be made in a hurry won't turn out good. At times I find myself acting like her or even doing some of the things she used to do, and it used to scare me. Now it just reassures me that all those years of teaching are paying off.

Deiadra S. Jones is a college student from Hot Springs, Arkansas.

Of Love and Discipline

BY JANET WEST SELLARS, FOR LEOLA "BUNNY" WEST

My girlfriends sometimes complain about their mothers and how they get on their nerves or try to instruct them on how to discipline "their" grandchildren. Somehow the rules seemed to have changed when it came to the new spawn. I actually miss those encounters with my mom now. She was a single parent and that was synonymous with no-nonsense parent in our house.

My mom, Leola "Bunny" West, worked two jobs and did not have a lot of time for foolishness from her children. I remember vividly how my mother believed that anytime a teacher sent a note home or made a phone call to her about me or my siblings' attitudes, the teacher was always right and we were always wrong.

Now mind you, my mom was a social worker. But that did not stop her from popping me upside my head if I got out of line in school or sassed her at home. And, she made sure we all knew that she was willing to go to jail for what she believed in. And to our chagrin, she believed in thumping her kids. As I look back on the many times I tested that concept, she held firm to her belief system. Once she even gave me a number to call if I felt I wanted to go into a foster home. Upon reflection, being the child of a social worker and knowing what I knew about foster care, beat-downs and all, my house was still the best deal in town.

As an adult, I was fortunate enough to have my mother's first grandchild. It was a sight to behold while I was in labor, as she questioned the doctors and nurses. When my labor wasn't progressing as they had hoped, they ordered a drug for me called Pitocin. My mother frowned and said, "Ya'll still use that?" But nothing compared to when my daughter actually made her entrance into the world. I remember my mother telling me that having her was the best thing I had ever done until that point in my life. I think what she was really telling me was that children were the most precious gift I'd ever receive. It was then that I realized that she believed we were gifts even when she was whipping the snot out of us. I also remember that moment being the first time she ever told me—at least in words—that she loved me. It was an awkward moment, but it marked a dramatic shift in our relationship.

As the years went on and we became closer and my daughter became the apple of Grandma's eye, I realized to what lengths she would go to protect her gene pool.

As I look back on all the moments with my mom, the whippings seem so inconsequential in the grand scheme of things. There are many in my generation who blame their parents for their shortcomings and failures in life. Some would even have the gall to say that I was adversely affected in some way because I was spanked as a child. I know, without a doubt, that I was loved beyond measure. My mom loved me enough to get my attention long before I had a chance to become a burden to society. I actually cared about her opinion of me and didn't want to disappoint her.

Sure I've spanked my kids every now and then. I'm not saying I black their eyes or break their bones, but a pop on their behinds to get their attention has made a difference, just as it did for me. And even though my mom would have cut her arm off before ever laying a hand on my daughter, I'm glad that my little girl, who's now twenty-three years old, got a chance to experience the security of being loved beyond measure before her grandmother went to sing with the angels.

Janet West Sellars is the author of Quiet As It's Kept. *She resides with her family in Newport News, VA, where she is working on her sophomore project,* Can't Let Go. *Visit her website at www.janetwestsellars.com.*

My mom, my nemesis
BY TOSCHIA, FOR VERDELL MOFFETT

I n life we can relate a lot of who we are and what we have accomplished to our teachers, peers, siblings and fathers. However, there is no relationship that is more poignant, more profound, than a child's relationship with their mother.

My mother has always been my biggest cheerleader, as well as my worst critic. As a young girl, when other students would rejoice with a "C" on their report card, I knew a "C" was not accepted in my home. Mom said, "If you are slow, then I will have you put in a lil' special class. Or if I feel that you are learning disabled, then I will put you on medication. Otherwise you'd better make the honor roll." And that is what I did! My mom would equally bestow tons of love, praise and accolades on me whenever I deserved it. I think Robert Fulghum's title *All I Really Need to Know in Life I Learned in Kindergarten* could have easily been changed to *All I Really Need to Know in Life I Learned from Mama*. An educator by profession, my mother taught me about humility and compassion. As a child, I was deemed an elitist, smart, spoiled brat. I had no tolerance for other children unless they were a "child prodigy" like myself. Even then my patience grew thin with my peers.

One particular incident helped to mold me into the person that I am today. I was eight years old. It was summertime and my mom was the local Girl Scout leader and our house was the neighborhood hangout. There was a girl whom I'll call Karen. We were both the same age and went to the same school. I noticed that her mother never showed up to any school functions or any Girl Scout activities. She would always be dropped off hours early and picked up hours late, and each time it would be by a different undesirable-looking person. My mom took a special liking to Karen and would always choose her to be the special helper with group activities. Then, Mom took it to a whole other level and let her help prepare snacks for the Girl Scout meetings. Back then, I was mean as hell. I was selfish and hated sharing my mother. Of course, Mom would ask me if I wanted to help out and I always said no. I was going to be the next Barbara Walters and didn't have time for menial tasks.

Karen started staying overnights sometimes on Saturday. I would hear my parents whispering about how sad it was that her mom hadn't packed her any underwear or fresh clothing.

One weekend I'd gone to stay with my grandparents and when I came home Karen was on my top bunk bed reading one of my Nancy Drew novels. I became incensed and told her I hated her and for her to find her own mama.

My mother immediately took me in her bedroom. That night I think I got the worst spanking of my life. I was told that not everybody had a family that loved them, doted over them like I did. Without saying too much, she said that some kids had a lot of problems; that's why they didn't want to stay at home. I rebutted that Karen said all the time how much money she had, who she knew, and what her mom was going to buy her. Mom just smiled and said, "People that brag about what they have and who they are are not happy. They are trying to convince themselves by lying." Mom's scolding ended with what I'll call my mantra: "To whom much is given, much is required." That phrase was what made me clerk at Legal Aid to help indigent people like Karen. That is what has catapulted me to volunteer with the "Rock The Vote" campaign, The National Democratic Party and my brief stint as a U.S. Senatorial page.

I later found out that poor Karen was, in fact, running. The next summer the biggest scandal in our town erupted. Her stepfather had sexually molested Karen from the age of six to nine years old. She finally confessed to her grandmother and was put into foster care. That is just one particular incident in my life that my mom was so wise that I will forever be amazed.

As a teenager, other kids would say what they wanted to be when they grew up. Mom, being the multi-faceted person that she was, constantly instilled in me not only the desire to learn, but has always made me feel like I can accomplish anything. I never had one thing that I wanted to be when I grew up. I was going to be a lawyer, political activist, writer and singer. My mother said, "Honey, you are a descendant of royalty so you can accomplish anything." Some may mistake Mom's advice as arrogance. I look at it as footprints. She suggested that I not only major in English but double major in Political Science, with a minor in music. That actually turned out well for me because if practicing law didn't work, then I could be a writer. Now, thanks to my cheerleader, I'm in negotiations for my debut jazz CD to be released in 2007.

All was not always good with Verdell, though. Sometimes she would just hurt your feelings and as much as you'd want to curse her out, you knew you couldn't. I remember coming home on break from college, and me and my girls were going out to the club. I had bought a new green outfit that was cute, or at least I thought it was. I walked into the den and asked my mom how I looked. She looked up from the book she was reading and said, "Like a lil' black leprechaun." Then when I scowled at her, she said, "Don't ask my opinion and I won't tell you." We looked at each other, busted out laughing and I changed clothes.

I owe all that I am to my mother, my nemesis, who continues to teach me about life. Recently I went to visit her classroom and tears came to my eyes as I saw all of these sixth-grade students so full of hope, clinging onto her every word. She was telling them, as she'd told me, about decisions in life. Her favorite poem for thirty-one years has always been "The Road Not Taken" by Robert Frost. The poem ends with what I want my children, all children to dream—and know—that anything is possible if you put God first and treat others the way you want to be treated.

Two roads diverged in a yellow wood, and I took the road less traveled by and it has made all the difference.

Mommy, I love you!

Toschia is a lawyer and author of You Wrong for That. *She resides in Killeen, TX. Check her out online at www.toschia.com.*

Home is where the heart is

BY NISAA SHOWELL, FOR ROSA LEE WARD-SHOWELL

I f home is truly where the heart is, then many mothers are cardiac specialists. We all crave the goodness of that maternal bond, which lasts, if you're lucky, a lifetime.

Nurturing mothers are their children's first teacher. From an eager baby learning to sing the alphabet song, to able-bodied women choosing the perfect wedding dress. That strong woman abiding with you through life cycles proves to be more than a biological gene pool. Anyone who can give you a kiss and put you on punishment in the same breath has to be more than a woman, and my mother is most definitely a paragon.

I remember one day when I was five, my two older sisters and I struggled to find our way home from grade school, traipsing ineffectively through the blizzard of '86. Our frostbitten limbs braved the storm as the blistery frigid wind stung our cheeks and noses. We traveled for hundreds of miles, (okay, it was only one city block), before I became consumed by the elements. I declared defeat and the crocodile tears began to pour. We all stood idle, frozen from freezing. Just as my sister Shari proclaimed, "We can make it!" Mommy appeared from the shadows, her loving expression fueled by anxiety and concern. Relieved, she rushed to us like a beacon of light carrying every hat, mitten and scarf cotton ever crafted. Just that small dose of her sweet tender care was enough to melt our icicle crusts. And that kind of selflessness is not uncommon for a vanguard leader.

Not only is Mrs. Rosa Showell the cornerstone role model for my siblings and me, she is the keynote for thousands of women and children in the tri-state area. Serving for over twenty years as an income maintenance caseworker, she is able to subsidize career placement and housing for underprivileged families who rely on county assistance. She never complains; she just does what she can, the best she can. I watch her in awe.

But wait, there's more to the full-time wife, mother and potent career woman. Now we can add graduate student to her repertoire. My mom was a member of Lincoln University's graduating class of 2003. With her Master's degree in hand, she was also inducted into the Pi Gamma Mu International Honor Society. Wow! We had never been so proud. I have a mother whose accomplishments on paper made reaching stars seem as easy as pie, square root not included. But what about the home front?

We were protected, not sheltered; cared for, but not spoiled. Values were instilled and we were trusted to make the right decisions. Morals were passed down and we knew someone was always watching. Oh, so you want to curse outside in the street? Neighbors from six houses away would beat your butt and then tell Mama. And you don't want it with Mama. My mother was far from abusive. She found a balance to commanding her home. With her, there were no excuses.

We are all extremely impressionable as adolescents, so there has to be a motivating force in your ear ten times greater than the voice of your peers and the voices streaming from the radio and television. For me, that voice has always been Mom.

Even when we didn't have much, my mom made sure we knew we would always have each other. Her efforts are epic and without bounds. She refuses to allow us to settle and drives us to stand for something, because if you don't stand for something you will fall for anything.

Nisaa Showell resides in Philadelphia. She is author of Eternal Souls Clashin'. *Visit her website at www.nisaashowell.com.*

I never needed another friend

BY LISA KEITH, FOR JILLIAN KEITH

In high school I was considered one of the coolest kids in school. That's because of my mother, Jillian Keith. She was everybody's friend. My house was where you could come hang out until the wee hours of the morning, where underage drinking and smoking were no big deal. In fact, if you caught her on a good night, my mother was the one fixing the drinks.

My mother always believed that teens were going to drink and smoke anyway, so they might as well do it where she could see them. She also believed teens would have sex anyway, so it was no big deal to let a boy spend the night in my room. Every one of my friends thought that was the coolest thing they'd ever seen. They couldn't understand why I didn't beam with pride whenever someone raved about my mother.

What my friends didn't understand—and neither did my mother—was that I had enough friends…I wanted a mother. I wanted someone to fuss because I stayed out past curfew. Shoot, I wanted a curfew. I wanted a mother who found weed in my backpack and tried to beat me into next week. I wanted a mother who got mad when I didn't clean my room, who berated me for not doing my homework, who wasn't passive about everything I did.

Everyone thought I was crazy, but I longed for my mother to fuss, scream, curse me out, go off on me, anything to act like she cared.

She never did get it. I wasn't a bad child, but I did things to get a reaction. Like the time I invited the whole neighborhood over for a party when she was supposed to be out of town. I'd found out that she would be returning early, but I went ahead with the party. I think deep down, I wanted her to put me on punishment, just do something. When my mother walked in that evening, she did voice shock at her house filled with people. When she found me in the basement cuddled up with a boy, I knew the time had come. She politely asked the boy to "give us a moment."

I waited for her to light into me. Instead she said, "Why didn't you tell me you were having a party?"

I was dumbfounded. But even more so because she then went upstairs and jumped into the *Soul Train* line.

I grew bitter toward my mother, and she never could understand that. To this day, she still doesn't. I could never understand my mother's way of showing love. And I do believe she loved me; it's just our idea of how you show that love differs greatly.

I've tried talking to my mother, to no avail. She likes the way she is. I'm her only child, and she says she never wanted to be one of those strict, domineering mothers. So instead, she became the total opposite.

My mother never understood I didn't want a mean mother just as I didn't want one who let me do what I wanted. I just wanted a happy medium. I never found it.

For years I have held my feelings inside. Now, I know that it's time for me to let go of that bitterness and move on. But before I do, I implore my mother and other mothers of the world like her to understand that despite all your good intentions, the child you bring into the world needs you to be a mother. We long for not only your love, but your discipline. It's okay to be a friend, but first and foremost, always be a mother.

Lisa Keith is a freelance writer in Miami, FL. She is at work on her first novel, Until the Dust Settles.

ABOUT THE AUTHOR

ReShonda Tate Billingsley is a general assignment reporter for KRIV, Fox 26 News in Houston, TX. The University of Texas at Austin graduate is the author of the *Essence* #1 Bestselling novel, *Let the Church Say Amen*. The motivational speaker/poet is also the author of *My Brother's Keeper, Four Degrees of Heat* (Anthology), *I Know I've Been Changed* (Feb. 2006), *Have a Little Faith* (Anthology- July 2006) (all published by Simon & Schuster/Pocket Books); as well as *Something to Say: Poetry to motivate the mind, body and spirit*. ReShonda is married with two daughters. Visit her website at www.reshondatatebillingsley.com.

SNEAK PREVIEW! EXCERPT FROM

I Know I've Been Changed

BY ReShonda Tate Billingsley

COMING FROM SIMON & SCHUSTER/POCKET BOOKS
FEBRUARY 2006

PROLOGUE
1995

I am outta here and I don't care if I never see this place again. Shondella, Reno, Auntie Mel. Even Mama Tee. I don't need none of them. Tell me I ain't gonna make it. I'll show 'em all. They can have this funky town.

Here I was, standing in front of Eddie's Filling Tank, the lone gas station/bus stop in town, with all my belongings stuffed into four tattered suitcases. There was no turning back, not that I'd even want to. I was tired of Sweet Poke and all that it *didn't* have to offer. The one-stoplight town didn't even have a movie theater or a mall. The only three stores in the town were the five-and-dime store; McConn's, an overpriced, old-people clothing store; and Piggly Wiggly. We didn't even have a freakin' Wal-Mart. If you wanted a decent pair of underwear you had to drive twenty minutes to the next town to get it. And the nearest major city, Little Rock, was an hour and a half away. Sweet Poke was simply not a place where you could thrive. And it definitely wasn't a place for someone like me.

Shondella, my jealous older sister, had laughed when I first announced my intentions to leave and go work in Tyler, Texas. She said I would probably end up hooking on the street. Then there was my great-aunt Mel, who had helped my grandmother raise me since my no-account mama decided she didn't want to be a mama anymore and left me, Shondella, and my twin sister and brother, Jasmine and Justin, at this very bus stop. Auntie Mel had prayed over me like I needed to be exorcised or something. Mama Tee wouldn't even say goodbye; she just acted like I was goin' to the corner store or something.

I glanced at my watch. The bus was over an hour late and the wind was kicking my tail, messing up the forty-dollar, spiral-curled hairstyle that I'd had to sleep sitting up to maintain. I couldn't have that. People were always telling me I looked like the former Miss America, Vanessa Williams, so I'd tried to copy this hairstyle she always wore.

I caught myself coughing as some of the dust being kicked around by the wind got lodged in my throat.

"Just another reason to get out of this place," I muttered. Sweet Poke, Arkansas, was known for its twister-like dirt clouds. And that about summed up all this town had to offer. On the list of progressive places in the country, Sweet Poke would rank at the very bottom. That's why I had to leave. Ever since I was in junior high school, I'd known I was bigger than this place. My family, friends, Reno, none of them could ever understand that. Some of my relatives called me uppity, but they just didn't understand. It wasn't only the slow pace that was driving me insane, but I simply couldn't live in poverty. Since the average salary in this town of three-thousand people was just over fourteen-thousand dollars a year, poverty was a very real option. Growing up, we were dirt poor, although you'd never know it because Mama Tee was always hollering 'bout we was rich in spirit. Yeah, right. Tell that to the light company. They ain't trying to hear nothin' 'bout no spirits.

No, my future would be nothing like my past. I refused to be like Mama Tee, struggling to make ends meet, yet still singing every church song in the book. Forget that. Don't get me wrong, I haven't completely stopped believing in God; I just don't think He makes frequent stops in Sweet Poke. If He did, everyone here wouldn't live such miserable lives.

I used to pray that God would make things better for us, that he would bring my mama back. That was a pipe dream. All the nights I cried, all the nights I prayed for hours, begging God to bring my mother back didn't make a bit of difference. I wanted my mother in my life so much I tried to bargain with God, saying stuff like I'd get straight A's and never trouble Mama Tee again if He would just bring her back. Yet, it never happened. So despite what Mama Tee is always saying, to me it don't look like God answers prayers. Least he ain't never answered none I sent up.

That's why I stopped waiting on God to change my situation and set out to change it myself. I was headed for bigger and better things. I was going to show the world that I wasn't some discarded little girl.

I pulled my scarf over my hair. I definitely didn't want any dirt getting in my hair. After I was sure I had it adjusted to where it was covering my entire head, I stepped out into the parking lot and peered down the road. "Finally," I mumbled as I noticed the big gray bus making its way through the clouds of dust.

For the first time that day, a smile crossed my face as I watched the Greyhound Bus pull into the service station. I wished that it would just slow down long enough for me to jump on board, then just keep going.

"Evening, Ma'am," the portly bus driver said as he stepped off the bus. "Will you be joining us?"

"Naw, I'm just standing out here in a dust storm for my health," I snapped.

The driver narrowed his eyes. "No need to get smart, little lady."

"No need to ask dumb questions." I was not in the mood for cordial exchanges. I was just anxious to get out of Sweet Poke, the place I'd called home most of my life. "Yes, William," I said, reading his nametag. "I'm waiting on you. I've been waiting for the last hour and a half." I thrust my ticket toward him.

William forced a smile and shook his head. "They don't pay me enough for this," he mumbled as he took the ticket.

"What?" I asked, my hands firmly planted on my hips.

"Nothing," William responded. "We'll be taking a five-minute break, then we'll be heading out."

"Fine." As irritated as I was, I had waited all my life for this. What was another five minutes?

The driver rolled his eyes, then made his way over to where my luggage sat and began loading it on the bus. My entire life, stuffed in four pieces of unmatching, frazzled luggage. One Samsonite I had borrowed from Auntie Mel and three cheap pieces that Mama Tee had probably gotten on sale at a thrift store.

I huffed and was just about to board the bus when I heard someone say, "So you really gon' do this? Raedella Rollins is really gonna just up and leave?"

I stopped and turned toward Reno, my boyfriend of six years. Make that ex-boyfriend. We broke up two months ago after I caught him coming out of the only motel in Sweet Poke with Ann Paxton, the town tramp. I was hurt by his actions, mostly because he knew in a town as small as Sweet Poke, he wouldn't be able to cheat and get away with it. Still, he did it anyway. In fact, it was my sister who had come running home, out of breath, to tell me Reno was at the motel. The motel clerk had called somebody, who called somebody, who called my sister. Since we mix like oil and water, Shondella took great pleasure in bringing me the news.

"I guess you thought I was joking," I responded as I made my way to the side of the bus where he was standing. "I told you, Reno, I'm outta here. I'm destined for bigger and better things."

"This is about Ann, isn't it? I told you she don't mean nothing. *She* kissed *me*." Reno smiled that crooked smile that had captured my heart when I was just a freshman in high school. His eyes twinkled as he stood there in his Dickie overalls, holding a can of Coca-Cola. I'd known Reno since I was a little girl. But he'd moved away after his parents divorced when he was nine years old. When he returned to live with his father, he came back a handsome young man who had every girl within a hundred miles of Sweet Poke feigning for him. Even now, he was as handsome as he was the day he first stepped foot in my freshman English class. His honey-brown complexion, short-cropped hair, enchanting eyes and deep dimples, almost made me think twice about my decision to leave. Almost.

"Whatever, Reno," I said, snapping out of the trance his eyes were luring me into. "That was your tongue down her throat, not the other way around. Anyway, I'm not going down that road with you again."

Reno displayed a big, cheesy grin. I used to believe Reno was one of the good guys. He was loving, attentive and honest, or so I thought. That's why his cheating hurt me so much. I never saw it coming. He tried to give me some line about Ann claiming she had dropped something down the sink in that motel room and needed his help to get it out. I told him he must think I was Boo-boo the fool if he expected me to believe that.

Reno reached out and tried to take my hand. "But we're a team. Always have been, always will be. Even when you tried to play hard and break up with me, I knew where your heart was. We belong together."

"Save that crap for your next victim," I said, jerking my hand away. "We broke up months ago. And this is about me. Wanting more than this two-bit town can offer. So Ann can have you because I don't want you."

"Tell that to someone who doesn't know you." Reno laughed, infuriating me.

"Let me explain something to you," I said, wiggling my neck. "You are a country bumpkin, low-down, stank dirty dog. That's why I wouldn't get back together with your broke behind. And you have no aspirations to leave this place. You're happy working your minimum wage job at the Railroad. But me...CNN is calling, baby." I stood with my head held high.

Reno narrowed his eyes, looking at me like I was crazy. "Shondella told me you're going to Tyler, Texas. That's a long way from CNN."

"But it's on the way!" I was sick of people degrading my decision to take a job as a reporter in Tyler. Auntie Mel said I was just jumping out of the frying pan and into the fire by leaving one small town to go to another. Both she and Mama Tee had blasted me for going away to a town where I didn't know a single soul. But I'd let my family talk me out of going away to college, even though I wanted desperately to leave this place. Between being broke and madly in love with Reno, I'd been suckered into commuting to college at The University of Arkansas at Conway, which was about thirty minutes from Sweet Poke. Still, I stayed focused, earning my degree in Broadcast Journalism and sending out audition tape after audition tape until I finally got a job offer in Tyler. "I have to pay some dues. Anyway, I'll only be there a few months before some big-time television station will snatch me up."

Reno doubled over with laughter.

"Forget you, Reno. You ain't gotta believe in me. That's why I'm leaving your country tail. And you will be sick when you see me on CNN, or *Entertainment Tonight* or *60 Minutes!*" His disbelief made me even more determined to fulfill my dream of becoming a nationally known news anchor.

"Yeah, right," Reno said between laughs. "You call me country? Your behind still talking 'bout 'can I *axe* you a question?' How you gon' be Barbara Walters and you can't even talk right?"

Reno eased his laughing and leaned in, running his hand across my face, which was on fire with fury. "Baby, face it. Sweet Poke is where you belong. You just a little ol' country girl. Your people are here," he stressed as he leaned in closer. "It's where you were born, where you gon' die. You can't run from it. It's in your blood."

His words made me shiver. This couldn't be my destiny. I'd get away from Sweet Poke or die trying.

"Lady, if you're catching this bus, you best get moving."

I hadn't even noticed the driver get back on the bus. I shook myself out of the trance Reno's words had put me in. I threw him one last scornful look. "We'll see who has the last laugh," I said.

With that, I turned and boarded the bus, leaving Reno standing in the midst of the dust storm.

Within minutes, I was settling into a seat near the front of the bus, where I leaned my head back. As the bus took off, I closed my eyes tightly. I refused to look out the window at Reno or Sweet Poke. All of that was my past. I was headed to my future.